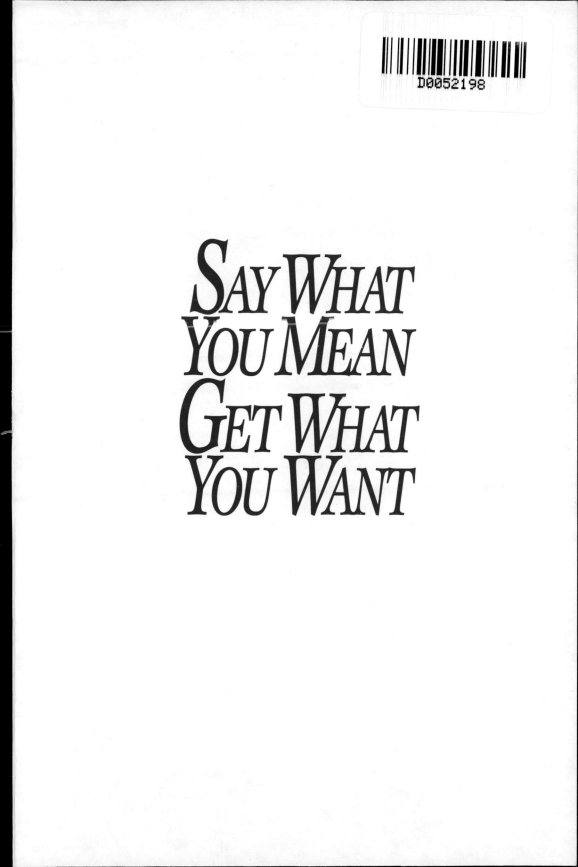

SAY WHAT YOU MEAN GET WHAT YOU WANT

Say What You Mean You Mean Get What You Want

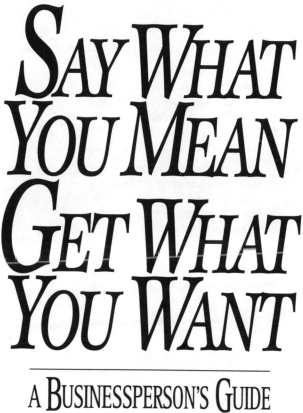

A Businessperson's Guide to Direct Communication

JUDITH C. TINGLEY, Ph.D.

American Management Association

New York • Atlanta • Boston • Chicago • Kansas City • San Francisco • Washington, D.C.
Brussels • Mexico City • Tokyo • Toronto

Library of Congress Cataloging-in-Publication Data

Tingley, Judith C.
    Say what you mean get what you want : a businessperson's
guide to direct communication / Judith C. Tingley.
        p.   cm.
    Includes bibliographical references and index.
    ISBN 0-8144-7904-9
    1. Business communication.   2. Communication in management.
3. Oral communication.   I. Title.
HF5718.T56   1996
658.4'5—dc20   95-51445
                                                              CIP

Printing number

10   9   8   7   6   5   4   3   2   1

Contents

Preface

Colleagues often say to me, "Are you still teaching assertive communication? I can't believe that people in the workplace of the nineties are really afraid to speak up. I thought assertiveness was long gone as a problem or as a trend." Open, direct communication may not be trendy, but right now, assertiveness is the valued communication style in the U.S. business culture. It's the infrastructure of good communication in the high-tech, high-speed, leaner, flatter organizations of today. Books about business, about organizations, and particularly books about teams continue to emphasize good, open, direct, and honest communication between individuals and groups as the key to success in the U.S. workplace of the nineties.

In the introduction to a 1975 book, *The New Assertive Woman*, Sheila Tobias says,

> Surely the right to be treated with respect, to have and to express feelings, opinions, and wants, to be listened to and taken seriously by other persons, to set one's own priorities, to say no without feeling guilty, and to get what one pays for are fundamental rights of human beings. It is amazing, but nonetheless necessary, that a book had to be written to tell women that they have such rights and to teach them how to ask for them.

The women that Tobias was talking about were the women who came to my early assertive communication classes; women who weren't sure they did have the right to ask for what they wanted, to say no, to express their opinions forcefully or directly. They were traditional women, playing stereotypical female roles and wanting above all to be nice and avoid confrontation.

Almost two decades later, the characteristics of the participants in my assertive communication classes and the nature of problem situations they bring have changed dramatically. Men as well as women are recognizing tremendous needs for improved communication skills at work. In the teamwork atmosphere of the nineties, men often need to tone down their formerly aggressive style and learn to speak in a less competitive, challenging, but still brief and direct way. The command-and-control, aggressive, sometimes harsh-and-punitive style of communication is no longer acceptable or desirable in the newer team-guided philosophy of U.S. business.

Male managers are seeing a continuing need to communicate clearly and concisely, but in a more collaborative rather than authoritarian way. They're seeing a need for a kinder, gentler approach that is direct without being intimidating. This awareness is triggered by the increased percentage of women and of male workers from less competitive cultures in the workplace that used to be mostly male and American. The lighter approach also works well with men of all ages and levels of seniority who are tired of feeling beaten up by the harsh communication of the old days and times.

Men are recognizing the importance of listening better, being more inclusive in their conversation, and moving toward communication that encourages participation on the part of their team members. Men are also finding that they need to better understand their own emotions as well as those of others in the people-oriented workplace. They need to be able to talk more directly about that touchy topic (for them): feelings.

Women, moving up the ranks of organizations or in entry-level positions, still often find themselves working primarily with men who want and expect more concise direct communication than many women are used to delivering. They also find that female colleagues in the workplace are placing more value on directness in delegating, running meetings, giving feedback, and giving instructions. No one wants or expects to take time for beating around the bush!

Both men and women are seeing the effects of the global marketplace, changing management philosophies, and increasing diversity in the workforce on their organization and their role. They're beginning to see that the old tried-and-true, traditional, competitive, aggressive, command-and-control communication that has been the hallmark of U.S. business for years is not acceptable to many other cultures. At a recent seminar I attended on marketing in Mexico, speakers unanimously pointed out that the normal business communication style of many U.S. businessmen is the kiss of death in Mexico. They had learned from experience that the word *macho*, though generally associated with the Mexican culture, doesn't apply to or permit aggressive business communication.

Now, in part as a result of value changes in the national and international workplace, both men and women see the need to develop assertive communication skills. Although overall women still comprise a larger percentage of attendees at my assertiveness workshops, their increased representation indicates a higher need for the skills of directness but also a greater level of self-awareness and willingness to learn, to change, and to adapt.

Men are more likely to wait for something dramatic to happen before they seek help in changing:

- They receive a poor performance appraisal.
- A significant person in their life tells them their communication is terrible.
- They don't get a wanted promotion or project assigned to them because of poor communication skills.

Most men and women in today's assertive communication classes are dealing with business communication problems, although some are dealing with both personal and professional problems. Some of the men are nonassertive, and some of the women are aggressive. Occasionally, both men and women are nonassertive and aggressive, bouncing back and forth between being too tough and too easy. In general, more men tend to be aggressive, and more women tend to be nonassertive.

Women generally can be direct and open in talking about feelings in personal relationships, but in the workplace, they are often uncomfortable and fear disapproval for being emotional, so they may express their feelings indirectly or stifle them. Men, on the other hand, often have difficulty being open and direct when it comes to talking about their feelings in personal relationships as well as in the workplace. Conventionally, the inability to express emotions has rarely resulted in a problem in the work environment. But in the emerging value system of the new workplace, the ability to identify, express, and communicate about feelings is high priority. Both men and women need to learn clear, concise, assertive ways to talk about their own and others' feelings at work.

Although men often can say "no" and express what they want, delegate, demand, and command, they may have difficulty in personal situations as well as in work situations coming across as a regular guy instead of a military leader when they are direct. Women may have difficulty saying "no" when friends and family ask for help as well as when they're asked to take on additional work or to stay overtime. Women often also have trouble telling others specifically what they want. They may have even more difficulty at work delegating assignments, giving clear directions and instructions, setting priorities for others, and giving negative feedback.

As the author of *Genderflex:*™ *Men and Women Speaking Each Other's Language at Work,* I've already made my views about men and women and their differences in communication very clear. For complex reasons having to do with socialization, testosterone, and brain structure, men and women are very different in the way they communicate. Men are perceived by both men and women as being more authoritative and domineering in their communication than women. And women are seen as people who don't speak up in business settings as often as they should.

When I ask groups of participants in my Genderflex™ workshops what is the one thing men need to do differently in their communication and what's the one thing that women need to do differently in their communication, the answer is always the same, coast to coast, north to south. Women say men need to listen and ask more and tell less, which I translate into: Be less aggressive and more assertive. Men say women need to speak up, to tell what they want, to get to the point, which I translate into: Be less nonassertive and more direct and assertive.

Realistically, women and men need to know how to communicate openly, directly, and honestly, without intimidating others and without feeling guilty or fearful. Men may more often have to move to that point from an aggressive, dominating stance, and women may more often have to move to that point from a more indirect, nonassertive position. But the ability to confidently rove the entire range of communication skills is necessary for men and women in today's diversity-oriented workplace.

J.T.

Introduction

I have a vivid memory of my early attempts at assertive communication. It was twenty-five years ago, give or take a year, and I was a nurse with a master's degree in psychiatric nursing. I had always had some difficulty with the "subservient" approach that seems de rigueur for nurses (generally all female) with doctors (generally all male). Plus, I was married to a physician who basically had the same thoughts about wives, at least at that time, that he did about nurses.

When I discovered assertive communication, my life changed. I saw that there was a way to be direct, open, and honest without being obnoxious. I realized I could express myself clearly and concisely without resorting to manipulation or intimidation. I was an immediate convert.

The physicians with whom I worked took the change easily and nodded their approval. The nurses that I associated with kept warning me that I would get in trouble, and when I didn't, they seemed annoyed. But most memorably, my physician husband one day commented to me, "Do you know what happens to assertive women?" I answered that I did not, and he said, "They end up divorced!" And, by gosh, I did end up divorced a few years later.

That may not seem too inspiring a message for readers who wish to acquire new or better ways of communicating, but fortunately times have changed. Certainly in business as well as in personal relationships and interactions, the need to communicate directly, openly, and honestly is evident.

Learning new ways to communicate effectively in the diverse workplace of the nineties can be as freeing an experience for you as it was for me twenty-five years ago. I have pursued a variety of different interests and consulting themes over the last seventeen years as a psychologist, but none has been quite as rewarding as teaching assertive communication.

Everyone changes. Participants take risks (feel free), gain confidence, and have fun. No one has regrets once they recover from their initial fear and start practicing. They find out that when they act and speak differently, they feel better, and then they can more easily continue to behave confidently, comfortably, and assertively. They're always sorry when the class ends, but vow to keep making progress!

SAY WHAT
YOU MEAN
GET WHAT
YOU WANT

1
You Gotta Do It

Good Communication

From my perspective, open, honest, and direct communication is an essential skill to hone, but it is only one form of good communication. There are a variety of important ingredients of good communication. One is adaptable, flexible communication, which means communication that is:

Sometimes direct and sometimes indirect
Sometimes subtle and sometimes hits like a sledgehammer
Sometimes entirely listening and other times entirely telling.

The basic cornerstone of all good communication in or out of the workplace is undoubtedly good listening. The second requisite skill is the open, honest, and direct style of communication, which has earned the title of assertive communication. Even in situations where being open, honest, and direct is not the technique of choice, knowing how to do it and knowing that you can do it gives you the confidence to choose another more indirect technique, a technique that would never have worked effectively for you unless you had the prior knowledge and comfort to be assertive.

History of Assertiveness

How did assertiveness start? Exactly what is it? Where did it go? Where is it going? And how does it fit with the workplace of the next century? The dictionary definition (*Webster's New World Dictionary*, 1984) of the verb *to assert* is: 1. to state positively; declare; affirm. 2. to maintain or defend (rights, claims, etc.). The credit for the development of training in assertive communication is generally given to Joseph Wolpe and Arnold Lazarus, whose book *Behavior Therapy Techniques* was published in 1966. As indicated by its subtitle, *A Guide to the Treatment of Neuroses*, it is an educational resource for therapists. On page 39, the authors say that assertiveness training is a useful treatment for people who respond with anxiety to a variety of interpersonal situations. Further, the authors state

... the term "assertive behavior" is used quite broadly to cover all socially acceptable expressions of personal rights and feelings. A polite refusal to accede to an unreasonable request; a genuine expression of praise, endearment, appreciation, or respect; an exclamation of joy, irritation, adulation, or disgust—may all be considered examples of assertive behavior.

A variety of societal changes that took place in the sixties also deserves credit for igniting the interest in assertiveness. These changes related to the added value that people began to place on personal relationships. Although improving, expanding, and strengthening relationships took on a new priority for many people, they often didn't have the communication skills to accomplish their interpersonal goals.

The sixties also established the beginning of a broader acceptance of differing ways of thinking, behaving, and living, at least in personal relationships. But people lacked the skills to act on their choices, to talk about their differences, and/or defend their choices. They needed a broader range of communication techniques and skills to accomplish their interpersonal goals. *Your Perfect Right: A Guide to Assertive Living*, by Robert Alberti and Michael Emmons, first published in 1970, presented the concepts of assertiveness training to the general reader, focusing primarily on personal communication. The book, long considered the bible of assertiveness, is still in print, but has changed its focus to deal with work as well as personal situations.

Assertiveness in the Nineties

The nineties continue to support an emphasis on effectiveness and development in personal relationships, but the increased focus on diversity in the workplace has generated a new outlook and an even greater pressure for improving working relationships. Peter Dailey points out in the June 1995 issue of *Managing Diversity* that communication plays a major role in creating successful interactions across lines of difference. "This [communication] is the most critical piece of the human-interaction puzzle!

And with well-intentioned people, it is the key to operating successfully in a diverse environment."

The business culture of the United States has continued to broaden the range of acceptability of differing lifestyles, differing ways of communicating, managing, and leading. Respect for the diversity of individuals and the importance of each person's own individual priorities has contributed to the acceptance of being more open in asking and telling about individuals' needs, wants, and values.

Clearly there's an even stronger need for open, direct, honest communication in the workplace of the nineties. Although assertive communication workshops now appear under a variety of titles such as "How to Manage Conflict," "How to Maintain Emotional Control," and "Dealing With Confrontation," most are still presenting the very useful basics of good old assertive communication. These workshops address issues such as:

- Keeping your cool
- Standing your ground
- Reaching positive solutions or holding your own in any situation with confidence and poise
- Expressing your ideas without alienating others
- Saying no
- Getting your point across without blowing up
- Earning others' respect
- Confronting people in a way that minimizes defensiveness and hostility

Everyone needs these skills at work, and they all are grounded in assertiveness.

What perhaps makes the communication needs of the workplace of the nineties different from that of previous decades (but not future decades) is that we all now need an ever-broader range of communication skills to deal with a greater variety of people and a wider spectrum of situations. There is not just one right way to deal with everyone and every situation. Some people and some situations necessitate an ability to communicate in an open, honest, and direct way. You need to have those assertive skills in your repertoire!

In the sixth edition of *Your Perfect Right,* Alberti and Emmons point out that assertive behavior in interpersonal relationships is primarily characteristic of Western cultures. They note that in Asian cultures, communication is often purposefully indirect so as to avoid confrontation or offense. The authors point out that just as Westerners need to learn to be comfortable with indirectness, perhaps Eastern cultures will need to learn to be comfortable with more directness in view of current international relations trends.

Communication competence is a characteristic that often determines who is promoted and who isn't. Although there is no clear, agreed-upon definition of what constitutes communication competence, Kreitner and Kinicki, in their book on organizational development, describe it as the individual's knowledge of when and how to use language in the social context. The authors describe research findings that indicate the use of assertive communication is more effective than aggressiveness in both work-related and consumer contexts.

Situational Assertiveness—When and Where It Works

Assertiveness is not always the communication approach of choice. But there are some clear indications for using open, honest, and direct techniques.

- People tell you that you need to be more direct.
- People tell you that you need to be more specific.
- People tell you that you need to be more concise.
- People tell you that they can't read your mind; they ask you to tell them what's on your mind.
- Many people don't seem to understand you.
- People are afraid of you or look intimidated by you.
- You often feel like a doormat.
- You often feel unappreciated.
- People don't do what you want them to do.
- Unfinished business with people whirls around in your

mind—sometimes for days after a conversation has concluded.
- You have a knot in your stomach, tension in your shoul-
ders, or headaches and backaches frequently.
- You've tried hinting, suggesting, wishing, telling someone
else, hoping they'd tell the target person—and it hasn't
accomplished what you'd like.
- The target person is an assertive communicator.

There are also a variety of situations where being open, honest,
and direct doesn't work well. You can presume a no-go when:

- You've tried a variety of assertive techniques before with
the target person, and they haven't worked. You haven't
felt better at the end of the conversation.
- The target person is extremely quiet, timid, or shy.
- The target person is very hostile and oppositional.
- The target person is from a culture that doesn't value
direct communication, or you're the minority person
working in a country that doesn't value direct, open communication.

Self-Assessment

Two different self-assessment tools follow to help you brain-
storm about what specific goals you want to accomplish as a
result of having read this book. Scoring instructions and inter-
pretations are included in a brief paragraph after the instrument.
In a more general sense, the first self-assessment tool, the Communication Scale, will help you determine where you are on
the continuum of assertiveness, aggressiveness, and nonassertiveness. The second, the Communication Survey, will help you
decide if you're more of a direct or indirect communicator. Then
you can decide if what you've got is what you want. If not, then
you can set goals that will facilitate your move from where you
are to where you want to be!

COMMUNICATION SCALE

This inventory is designed to provide information about the way in which you express yourself. Please put a number on the line following the question to describe how you usually express yourself in that particular situation. Your answer should not reflect how you feel you ought to act or how you would like to act.

0   Almost or always
1   Usually
2   Sometimes
3   Seldom
4   Never or rarely

1. Do you ignore it when someone pushes in front of you in line? _____
2. Do you raise your voice when you are trying to make a point in conversation? _____
3. Do you find it difficult to accept compliments from your boss or supervisor? _____
4. Do you think of yourself or do others think of you as having a temper? _____
5. Do you find it difficult to ask a friend to do a favor? _____
6. When someone criticizes you, do you quickly find something to criticize them about? _____
7. Do you keep information or opinions to yourself in discussions with people whom you do not know very well? _____
8. Do you feel that some people (family and/or friends) are afraid of you? _____
9. If you are angry at someone, is it difficult for you to tell them? _____
10. Are you sarcastic with other people? _____
11. Do you find it difficult to refuse people's requests? _____
12. Do you think up smart remarks and quick comebacks to put other people down or on the defensive? _____
13. Do you let other people make decisions about where to go and what to do? _____

14. If someone disagrees with you, do you strongly dispute their viewpoint? ____

15. Do you tend to drag out apologies? ____

16. Are you pretty sure you are right? ____

17. Is it hard for you to express your negative feelings to others? ____

18. Do you tell people your thoughts and opinions about their behavior when they don't ask you? ____

19. If you are angry at someone, is it difficult for you to tell him or her? ____

20. Do you tend to be judgmental about other people? ____

Score the odd-numbered questions separately from the even-numbered questions so that you come up with two totals: a total of your answers to odd-numbered questions, and a total of your answers to even-numbered questions. If your score for the even-numbered questions is between 0 and 10, you are generally not aggressive. If you score is between 31 and 40, you are generally aggressive. In between is in between! If your score for the odd-numbered questions is between 0 and 10, you are generally nonassertive. If your total score is between 31 and 40, you're generally assertive. If your score is in between, so are you!

COMMUNICATION SURVEY

Please circle the number that best indicates your behavior on the continuum accompanying each item.

1. When I want someone to do something, I use indirect means such as hinting.

    Hinting   1   2   3   4   5   Not hinting

2. When I express an opinion, I hedge it rather than state it flatly.

    Hedge   1   2   3   4   5   Flat out

3. I avoid saying anything to coworkers who have not completed assigned tasks on time.

    Avoid   1   2   3   4   5   Speak out

4. I believe others don't pay much attention to my ideas.

    Often   1   2   3   4   5   Seldom

5. I usually go along with other people's suggestions rather than they tend to follow mine.

    Go along   1   2   3   4   5   Follow me

6. I am concerned about my communication and do not feel confident to talk about whatever comes to mind.

    Concerned   1   2   3   4   5   Feel confident

7. I think I am a good listener.

    Yes   1   2   3   4   5   Not particularly

8. It seems I have to ask several times for people to do something for me.

    Often   1   2   3   4   5   Seldom

9. I think people interrupt me more than they interrupt others.

    Often   1   2   3   4   5   Seldom

10. In a meeting, I am the person who points out that the discussion has wandered off the topic.

    Seldom   1   2   3   4   5   Often

11. When I bring up an idea, others usually pick it up.

    Seldom   1   2   3   4   5   Often

12. People give me unsolicited advice on how to do my work.

    Often   1   2   3   4   5   Seldom

13. I try to express my opinion carefully so that others will not be offended.

    Often   1   2   3   4   5   Seldom

14. When others disagree with me, I try to find a compromise rather than try to argue them over to my viewpoint.

    Compromise 1   2   3   4   5   Argue

15. I use expressions such as "I want . . ." and "I think . . ." rather than say "It would be best . . ." or "A good idea might be . . .".

    A good idea 1   2   3   4   5   I want . . .

16. When my supervisor or manager asks for opinions from my group, I wait until others have spoken first.

    Seldom   1   2   3   4   5   Often

17. When I have a conflict with a coworker, I take the initiative to discuss it with the person.

    Seldom   1   2   3   4   5   Often

18. I begin a statement by saying, "This might be wrong, but . . ." or "You probably won't agree . . ."

    Often   1   2   3   4   5   Seldom

Score yourself: _____ Total of the circled numbers

The lowest possible score is 18, the highest, 90. The midpoint is 54. Low scores indicate indirectness, high scores indicate directness, middle scores indicate that you have indirect and direct communication skills.

Adapted from Jeffrey Eisen, Ph.D., *Powertalk! How to Speak It, Think It, Use It* (New York: Simon & Schuster, 1986).

Now that you know where you're starting from and why you want or need to change, move on to the next chapter to learn about the I Mean Business Modus Operandi for enhancing your communication skills and confidence.

2

Seven Steps for Effective Communication

The IMB MO is a seven-step system for becoming a more effective communicator.

1. Decide what you want
2. Identify negative thinking
3. Substitute, challenge, and stop
4. Select a technique(s)
5. Implement technique(s)
6. Reward yourself
7. Evaluate your effectiveness

Actually, the IMB MO can be used to guide you to do just about anything: be a volleyball champion, fix up your house, go back to college, write a book, or find a new job. For the purpose of this book, the IMB MO is aimed at improving communication on the job and attaining what you want as an outcome in any given workplace conversation or interaction.

Men and women in the workplace often ask me, as a communication consultant, a broad variety of questions:

"How can I have my thoughts and comments taken seriously?"
"What can I say to impress my boss?"
"How can I come across more confidently?"
"Why does my boss tell me I'm not a good team player and how can I get to be one?"
"How do I motivate people to do what I want them to do?"
"There are people who don't like me. How can I win them over?"

People also seek suggestions about handling a particular communication situation. For example:

"Should I ask Tom to help me with this project, or should I wait for him to offer to work on it?"
"Should I say something to my boss about his questioning my sick days or should I let it go?"
"Would it be better to answer all my boss's questions, even

> though I feel interrogated, or to change the subject, or to
> talk about his interrogating me?"

The answer to all of those questions is the same. It depends on
what you want.

Identifying what you want as the outcome of any interaction is the most important step in the process of learning how to
better manage your communication. If you don't accomplish
this essential first step, then you have a continuing problem, but
you don't have any possible solutions. For example, you may
not get along well with Jim, a coworker. He seems to avoid you,
has little eye contact with you, answers your questions with
brief answers and few details, and rarely joins a group that
you're in. That's a problem for you. Until you know clearly what
you want, there's no point in trying to figure out how to solve
the problem. You could want many differing outcomes: to understand him, to not take his behavior personally, to find out if
you should take it personally, or to tell him that you'd like him
to change his behavior. Obviously, what you're going to say or
not say will be determined by what you decide you want for an
outcome of the conversation, the situation, or the relationship.

If you decide that you want to understand him, then you
might say: "Jim, I'd like to set up lunch one day next week. I'd
like to get to know you and I'd like you to get to know me
a little better since we will be working more together on the
supervisory skills training." If what you want instead is to be
able to take his behavior less personally, then you say to yourself, "He's telling me something about him, he's not telling me
something about me." Then his behavior becomes less con-
nected to you, becomes less of a personal thing and more of a
communication problem that he has. Once you change what you
say to yourself, you can see that part of the accountability rests
with him, rather than all of it resting with you. So, instead of
thinking "What have I done wrong?" or "Why doesn't he like
me?", you can recognize that maybe he doesn't have good social
skills or he may be uncomfortable in unstructured work situations.

If you want to know whether you should take it personally,
then you approach the situation entirely differently. You could

tell him: "I'm concerned about the fact that we seem to have almost no working relationship, Jim. I'd prefer to have more communication between us. I'd also like to know your thoughts about the situation." If you want to be even more direct and tell him that you'd like a more communicative relationship, then you'd say, "I feel uncomfortable about the fact that we barely talk to each other at work. I'd like to spend more time together, talking on a regular basis."

Translating your problem into a goal transports you. Let's say your house is old and dilapidated looking. You can spend a lifetime talking about how tacky your house is—how it's falling apart, the rug is wearing out, the tile is getting chipped, the roof is leaking, and the paint is dingy. Until you translate all those problems into a want, nothing happens.

Once you decide what you want, then action takes place. Maybe you want to sell your house, or rent it and buy another house, or get a loan and fix it up, or gut it and remodel. But until you turn the problem into a goal, there's nowhere to go. That's why deciding what you want is the first and most important step in improving communication. Otherwise you stay stuck with the problem: He never talks to me. She's unfriendly. He doesn't understand me. She's intimidating. When you have a better idea of what you want as an outcome of a problem situation, then you're headed in the right direction. There may be other obstacles along the way, but without a clear, specific goal, you can't even start solving the problem. That's why determining what you want is the critical first step in the I Mean Business Modus Operandi.

Decide What You Want

Give some thought right now to what you want to be able to do differently when you've finished reading this book. I use a particular formula for stating goals in my communication workshops: I want to be able to _____, followed by the specific behavior, with the specific person(s), in the specific situation. For example, a goal could be: I want to be able to tell Steve that I'm overloaded and don't want to take on any new responsibilities when he asks me to do more. The advantages of having such a clear, specific goal are twofold. First, it's clear to you exactly what you want to do. Second, it's very easy for you to know when you accomplish that goal. I'd like to get along better with my coworkers is a vague, general goal. Knowing exactly how to start and what to do is unclear. Determining if and when you've accomplished the goal is cloudy. But when you have set a specific goal, you have clear direction about how to start, and you'll know when you've accomplished the goal.

Here are two goals, dissected according to the formula:

I want to be able to tell Michael that I don't like it when he hugs me at business meetings. I'd like him to stop.
I want to be able to _____.

Specific behavior:	tell that I don't like being hugged
Specific person:	Michael
Specific situation:	at business meetings.

I want to be able to tell Sandra not to come to me any more with her personal problems unless she wants to listen to me and take my advice.
I want to be able to _____.

Specific behavior:	tell that I don't want to spend a lot of time on personal problems
Specific person:	Sandra
Specific situation:	when she doesn't want to listen or take my advice

Some of the goals that past participants in my assertive communication classes have set are to:

- Tell people who put pressure on me about finding a job that I have a plan and am going to stick to it.

- Respond when my boss blames me for something I didn't do, rather than stewing about it and staying quiet.
- Tell my friend that I don't like it when he is sarcastic and says things that hurt my feelings.
- Tell people to do their own problem solving rather than involving me when it's their job to do it, not mine.
- Delegate tasks clearly to people at work when I am in the managerial position.
- Restate and stick to my position in a disagreement without coming across in a hostile, aggressive manner.
- Give negative feedback to a coworker, boss, or subordinate without sounding too harsh.
- Stand up for myself and what I want instead of always giving in to the wishes of others and telling myself it isn't really important.
- Give instructions to people in a clear enough way that they understand and can do what I need them to do.

None of these goals may be exactly what you want and need to do differently, but before you proceed, give some thoughts to three goals that you have, write them down, and keep them in mind as you continue to read. You'll find very specific steps to the accomplishment of your goals in the rest of this chapter.

I want to be able to:

Specific behavior: _____

_____

_____

Specific person or persons: _____

_____

_____

Specific situation: _____

_____

_____

Identify Negative Thinking

After you decide what you want, the next critical step is to determine if some negative thinking might get in your way. We all have an internal dialogue or monologue going on in our head most of the time, directing us how to drive the car or play tennis, how to act in a new situation, how to phrase a request or make a presentation to a group. Sometimes the internal conversation is loud, sometimes soft. Sometimes it seems to be occurring on an almost subconscious level and other times it seems as if someone is yelling at you inside your head. (You're still sane. It happens fairly frequently to normal people.) Whatever the circumstance, the internal conversation is a powerful factor in influencing how you communicate and how you behave.

People's internal conversation usually falls into one of three categories:

- I'm not good enough.
- You're not OK.
- Why bother? Nothing'll change anyway.

There are Olympic-caliber negative thinkers who can fall into all three of these categories, sequentially or at the same time. The first pattern, I'm not good enough, refers to a pattern of thinking where most of the internal conversation involves putting oneself down in various ways. Perhaps you've disagreed with a co-worker, Selena, on the best way to accomplish a task. You did it your way, but since then, you can feel the tension between you. You'd like to say something to her, but you're afraid. When you're thinking about communicating directly with Selena, your internal monologue might sound like this:

"I'll sound like an idiot. I'm going to stumble over my words, and not say it right."

"I know I'll hurt her feelings and then she'll always be mad at me."

"I should just let this go. I'm being oversensitive by even letting it bother me. As usual, I'm making a mountain out of a molehill. I should never have let it go this far anyway."

With that kind of mental dialogue, there's almost no way that you can get yourself to say what you want to say, even if you do know what you want as the outcome.

The second type of internal negative thinking, You're not OK, has variations as well. Some typical negative thinking of this kind sounds like:

> "He's always screwing up, the jerk. He deserves to get reamed."
> "She's wrong, I'm right, so that gives me the right to sock it to her."
> "It's all their fault, not mine."

When the tone of the mind's monologue is blaming, or right-wrong, good-bad, win-lose, coming across with a direct comment that doesn't put the person down is unlikely. You almost inevitably sound negative or judgmental. The subtle or not-subtle anger underlying the communication delivers the message that you really aren't interested in improving communication or the relationship.

The third type of negative thinking focuses on a kind of passive resignation that evokes inaction:

> "There's no point in even trying. She won't listen anyway."
> "Things never change, so why bother?"
> "It doesn't really matter one way or the other."

With that kind of internal commentary going on, the individual usually does nothing, although she may still feel frustrated, angry, or uncomfortable about the person or situation that's bugging her.

Substitute, Challenge, and Stop

The next step in the IMB MO is so critical that it necessitates an entire chapter, Chapter 3. Once you have a goal and you're able to identify and easily recognize your own internal monologue, then you have to figure out a way to determine the barriers to success and to change the monologue. All three types of thinking listed previously are negative in the sense that they interfere with your being able to say and do what you want. When you change the commentary in your head, you can get on with the outer conversation that you need to have so that you can accomplish the outcome you want. This step is tough because you're usually breaking a long-standing habit. The various different methods you can use to alter your internal monologue are identified and described in Chapter 3, which contains concepts critical to becoming more assertive.

Select a Technique

Once you have erased and replaced your negative thinking, then it's time to decide which communication technique is going to work best in this particular situation with this particular person. Maybe you'll choose one or two ideas or a combination of techniques to use as ways of achieving the outcomes you want. When you're new at the IMB MO, writing a script or saying what you want to say in front of a mirror raises your confidence before the actual event. Practicing with a communication buddy playing the role of the other person (the target person) also increases your success ratio. Role playing with a pal is useful for phone conversation communication as well as in-person conversations. There's no doubt that behavioral rehearsal increases the likelihood that what you want to say will in fact come out the way you want it to in the real situation. Another useful practice situation is for you to role play the target person and for your communication buddy to be you, and see what it feels like as the target person receiving the differing communication techniques. Using this practice approach also can help you to see the real consequences of your communication on the target person, rather than just seeing your fears about the reaction of the target person.

Implement the Technique

Just doing it can be the second most difficult step, after the hardest task of stopping, substituting, and challenging your negative thinking. One of the useful mind games to play is to run movies in your mind of the difficult situations you've been in or that you anticipate being in, and think about how you might have dealt with it, or could have dealt with it, or will deal with it. See nice mental pictures of you being successful at dealing with interruptions, or saying no, or delegating responsibility. Visualizing increases your preparedness to interact assertively. Another important requirement to implementing a technique, any technique, is to expect imperfection. The first or second time you deal with a difficult issue and use some of the communication techniques that are new to you, they won't work fabulously and neither will you. You don't want to start with the most formidable situation or the most intimidating person. You want to build a history of success, which means that you start out implementing a simple (for you) technique, in a forgiving, noncritical situation with a pleasant person. Then you move on to using techniques or combinations of techniques that are more challenging for you in more touchy situations with more intimidating people. The goal is not to prove that you can quickly and easily vault huge mountains with a single leap, but that you can slowly and gradually take on increasingly complex communication tasks and feel good about how you've handled the situation.

Reward Yourself

The IMB MO takes a slight jog here from what you might expect. Whether you score a perfect 10 when you try out your chosen communication technique or whether you fail miserably, reward yourself for taking the risk, for attempting a different approach, for practicing your skills. The reward is not for success, it's for taking action! No action, no learning. No learning, no change.

The reward can be as simple as the relief you feel when a dreaded conversation is over. It can vary from a pat on your own back to an internal or external verbal praising, to telling someone else how terrific you are and asking them for validation and reinforcement, to buying yourself anything from a hot fudge sundae to a new car. It depends on how good you feel about what you did!

Evaluate Your Effectiveness

After you've rewarded yourself for doing what you wanted to do systematically and with a plan, then you can look back and determine how effective you were at doing what you wanted to do. You can review how the interaction went, or you can run it by someone else who understands the situation and is a good communicator, or you can occasionally ask the person to whom the comments or responses were directed about their reaction and what they thought. Whatever you choose, always add your own opinions to the others you have gathered, because how you felt and what your reaction was are essential components of determining if you did what you wanted to do, in the way you wanted to do it, and if it worked.

If your conclusion is that you handled it well, tuck the information away to use in other similar situations with other similar people. Maybe you'd benefit from keeping a communication journal for a while, documenting for yourself what techniques worked, with whom, and how you motivated yourself to do what you wanted to do.

If your approach didn't work, then give some thought to what you could have done differently, how you could have done it, what kept you from doing it in the first place, and how you might do it differently next time. And then, let it go. As one of the men in my assertive communication class recently said, the best motivational technique he has learned to use when he doesn't handle things well is to say to himself simply, "Next time!" I think that's a great idea.

3

What Are the Barriers?

Once you decide what you want as your communication outcomes and you're familiar with the IMB MO, you need to look at what might possibly get in your way of doing what you want to do. If there are no barriers, then you don't even have to finish reading this book. You can just go out and do whatever you want to do. But for most of us, many different obstacles hinder us from doing what we want to do, whether that's building a house, learning to play golf, or improving communication skills at work.

In the assertive communication workshops, I always ask people to observe themselves in their goal situation. I tell them not to actually do anything different than they usually do, but just to notice their feelings and their thoughts as well as their behavior. Then, determine for themselves as individuals with their target person in that particular situation what it is that keeps them from doing what they want to do. Repeatedly, in all my workshops with a broad diversity of participants, the biggest barrier to communicating assertively is fear: of being rejected, of change, of the unknown, of confrontation, of being the focus of attention, of hurting someone's feelings, of getting stressed out and ending up feeling miserable, of being viewed as mean or not a nice person, of fumbling or bumbling their words and sentences.

There's always fear of being intimidated, fear of not knowing what to say next if someone doesn't respond positively to your assertion, fear of losing control, or power, or status, or fear of losing a friendship or relationship. These fears are most commonly present in the "I'm not good enough" internal monologue. A second common pattern, representative of the "Why bother?" internal monologue of participants, is the barrier that is erected by thinking what you do won't make any difference anyway. The third theme that gets in people's way of communicating more assertively in the accomplishment of their goals is an outlook that emphasizes blame: the "You're not OK" internal monologue. The first two groups of people end up being nonassertive even though they come from different positions. The third type of person usually comes across as aggressive. For all three types of negative thinker, their internal monologue may be the biggest barrier to good communication.

There are also situations where at one time, with one person, you think, "Why bother? Nothing will change." Another time, with a different target individual, you might think, "I'm afraid of hurting his feelings. I better not say anything." And in yet another situation you might say to yourself, "That's the last straw. I won't put up with that garbage. He deserves to get shot down, put down, and beaten up, the jerk." All those different internal conversations of course will cause you to feel different ways, to behave in different ways, and to communicate in different ways.

Other obstacles get in the way of being a good, open, direct, communicator —obstacles that have less to do with fear than with real life consequences of being more direct and open. There's concern about getting fired or of losing a deal and income. There's concern about a relationship ending, about not getting a promotion, about getting divorced. For example, if you tell your boss assertively that you don't like his management style, you think he's ineffective, and you don't like working for him, your working relationship with him will probably suffer. There definitely could be real consequences.

Contrary to the example, my experience is generally that what people fear as a real consequence is often their negative thinking showing up in another form. Rarely do individuals have evidence that what they think will happen will in fact happen. For example, years ago I was doing an all-day seminar with about 125 people who were working for a large government organization. I was talking to them about assertive communication and suggested that if they were unhappy with a certain co-worker, supervisor, or a particular policy or procedure, that they had many options for discussing their concern openly and honestly with someone in management or human resources.

The group's response to me was that I obviously didn't really know the organization because you just couldn't do that kind of communicating. If you did, you would be written up for insubordination. I was surprised. That seemed archaic and my earlier conversations with upper level management had not led me to believe that the management style was quite that autocratic. But, not being certain, I thought I'd better check. I asked the group how many people had been written up for insubordination. No one raised a hand. I asked how many people knew someone who wasn't attending the workshop who had been written up for insubordination. Again, no hands went up. I asked how long the participants had worked for this organization. Many had been there for ten, fifteen, and twenty years. I asked if anyone attending had ever known anyone who had been written up for insubordination. No one did. In this instance, although people believed that what was keeping them from doing what they wanted to do was a real consequence, in fact it was a negative thought.

After discussing the barriers with thousands of people in a variety of settings, I've concluded that there are four main barriers to doing what you want to do:

- You don't know what you want; you haven't yet translated the problem into a goal.
- Negative thinking, like all those fears mentioned previously.
- You don't know how to do what you want to do. I may want to express my feelings directly, but if I don't know how, it won't happen.
- The real consequences. Sometimes being open, direct, and honest can definitely result in something happening that you don't want.

As mentioned in Chapter 2, not knowing what you want is definitely the barrier that keeps many people stuck in the problem. Women, more frequently than men, have a tendency to stay mired in the feelings and problems of a situation rather than thinking about, acting, and communicating about what they want in a specific and concrete manner.

In my current assertiveness class, one participant, Alma, said, "I'm so tired of my husband scaring me to death by always threatening to quit his job. He's so moody, always up and down. I never know what to expect. One day he says he'll quit his job. The next day he says his job is going great." When I pressed her to tell me what she wanted from him, she answered, "Peace and harmony." I asked her what peace and harmony looked like and sounded like. One of the men in the class said he would have no idea how to deliver peace and harmony to Alma if he were her husband, even if he wanted to. His comment helped her to think more concretely and specifically and add, "I want you to stop telling me you're going to quit your job. If you have those feelings, I'd like you to keep it to yourself, or tell other people, but not me."

Negative Thinking

Once you have the want clearly in mind, the next biggest barrier the negative thinking comes into play. To continue with the example just mentioned, when Alma finally became clear about what she wanted, her next thought, which she almost said out loud and immediately, was, "But he doesn't have anyone else to talk to and I'd probably hurt his feelings if I said that I didn't want to hear his complaints." Even when Alma knows what she wants, and even if she knows how to say what she wants to say, as long as she's thinking those thoughts about being afraid and being responsible for the other person, she probably will never do what she wants to do. Alma can learn how to alter those internal thoughts so they no longer are a barrier to doing what she wants.

Our internal dialogue or inner speech, the conversation that goes on in our head at all times, is possibly the most important determinant of how we feel and, consequently, how we behave. Early research by Donald Meichenbaum and other psychologists studying our thinking patterns demonstrated that becoming aware of the internal speech and learning to give yourself better instructions increased the likelihood of behaving in a desired way.

Many complexities are embedded in the relationship between an individual's internal thoughts and his or her ultimate behavior, but current psychological theory holds that changing internal thoughts can be a potent contributor to changing behavior and therefore to changing communication. Teaching people how to restructure their internal speech serves as the basis for bringing about change in individuals, groups, and organizations.

Cognitive Restructuring

You can change what you're saying to yourself in a variety of ways. Different approaches work for different people. *Cognitive restructuring* is a psychological term that refers to altering (or restructuring) our thoughts (or cognitions). It's the simplest way to change our internal monologue when that monologue is getting in our way of doing what we want to do. Perhaps you're in a situation where you want to tell your boss that his style of delivering negative feedback to you seems overly harsh and too public. Your internal monologue sounds like this: "I can't say that to him. He'll get really mad and be even nastier." The negative thinking has to be altered to more neutral thinking so you can move yourself toward speaking up to him. You use the process of cognitive structuring to find a neutral, substitute statement that you can use instead. "I'll start with a simple situation first," or "I can do this, one step at a time," or "I can feel the fear and do it anyway" are the products of the process of changing your thoughts. If you're a compulsive negative thinker or have been in the negative thinking habit for years, you probably will need to try a variety of ways to change your internal dialogue in addition to cognitive restructuring. Then continue to use those that work best for you.

The most important outcome of cognitive restructuring is getting rid of the negative thinking, even if it means reciting the Gettysburg Address to yourself to block out the negativity. Not-negative thinking is different from positive thinking. As a matter of fact, you can be as messed up being an overly positive thinker as you can by being an overly negative thinker, but in a different way. For example, if you say to yourself, "Everything will be fine. I know things work out for the best and this will too. I'll be rich and famous and live happily ever after," then sometimes you don't do what you need to do to achieve your desired result. You're out of touch with reality as a positive thinker but in a different way than as a negative thinker.

The antidote to both negative and positive thinking is just plain old realistic thinking, giving yourself better instructions. Think about driving your car. When you approach an intersection and the light turns from green to yellow, you don't turn into a negative thinker and say, "Oh, this is terrible. The light has changed. How could this happen? This is a disaster." Nor do you say to yourself, "This is wonderful. The light has changed. What a challenge!" Instead, you give yourself very good instructions. You say to yourself, "The light has changed. I need to look quickly behind me and in both directions coming toward me and figure out if it's best to slam on my brakes and screech to a stop or if it's best to roar across the intersection because getting rear-ended looks like a likely risk." That entire conversation takes place on an almost automatic level in a split second, but nonetheless, it does take place and each individual has his or her own level of awareness of the ongoing monologue.

The negative thinking adjustment is one we all have to make, in a variety of situations, not just learning to be a better communicator. When I'm driving to give a speech, I might find myself feeling nervous. When I check into my head I discover that what I'm saying to myself is, "Supposing I bomb," "Maybe they're not going to like me." Obviously as long as I keep up that pattern of thinking, I'm not going to be a hit. As soon as I open my mouth for this audience, even before I open my mouth, I'm going to look and sound insecure, nervous, and needy. That feeling, conveyed unchecked, will result in my actually being a bomb. On the other hand, if I say to myself, "I'm going to be a star. They'll love me and think I'm fabulous," I can run into another kind of problem. I can feel overly confident, not do the last-minute mental and psychological preparation I need to do for fine-tuning my presentation, and perhaps come across as cocky or cavalier.

The best approach for me is to recognize the negativity and substitute a neutral, realistic statement or just give myself better instructions. An example of the former would be to say to myself, "I'm experienced and I can handle this well." An example of the latter would be, "Take a deep breath, count to three, and let go. Stay calm and you'll be OK."

Here's a list of the kinds of negative internal monologues that were going on for the participants in a recent assertive communication class:

"I can't say no to her. She's my boss."

"He'll be very upset if I bring up old problems."

"If I'm dependent on them financially, I can't open my mouth about what I think or what I want."

"I just can't listen. I don't know what's wrong with me. Something must be wrong that I'm such a lousy listener. I lost my job last time because I didn't listen. Maybe I'll lose this job too."

"I have to live up to his expectations at all times, even if they seem unrealistic to me."

"I might hurt his feelings."

Coping Statements

When I pointed out the need to eliminate the negative thinking and substitute some coping statements, whether customized for them, by them, or taken full-blown from a menu, workshop participants were quickly able to come up with a variety of new self-statements that would work well for them. They substituted the new self-statements for the old self-defeating statements they were used to saying. Here's a brief sample:

"I don't get paid enough to put up with this garbage."

"I've survived this and worse before."

"I'm not going to break a sweat."

"Just one thing at a time."

"I'm an equal in this office."

"I have the right to say no."

"I have a responsibility toward him, but I'm not responsible for him."

These coping statements are all customized by the participants to fit a specific situation. Tailor-making your own coping statement increases its effectiveness, but borrowing one works well too. In the Appendix you'll find lists of coping statements or substitute statements that you can use instead of the pattern of negative self-talk that you already use. Try something different. The worst thing that can possibly happen is that it doesn't work either.

Reframing

You can use a variety of other ways to change your internal dialogue besides cognitive restructuring. Reframing is a very powerful and often quicker way to change your negative thinking. The word *reframing*, as I'm using it here, comes from the literature on neurolinguistic program, an approach sometimes used in psychotherapy, and refers to thinking differently about something or someone. Richard Bandler and John Grinder, authors of *Reframing*, say that reframing is changing the frame in which a person perceives events in order to change the meaning. They add, "When the meaning changes, the person's responses and behaviors also change." Changing the meaning implies thinking differently. It involves a large-scale change in the internal monologue. That's how reframing can help people communicate differently.

A classic example is often used in sales training. Sales people typically are fearful of rejection. Being told "no" is what sales people don't want. No is a negative, is bad, unwanted, undesirable, and rejecting. But, in sales training, a reframing technique is used to change the frame in which a no is perceived. Trainees are told that it often takes fifty noes to get a yes. Their task, then, is to go out and see who can get the most noes in the next four hours. Suddenly, noes become wanted, valued, and desirable. They become positive instead of negative in this reframing process.

Similarly, an individual can use reframing to alter the internal monologue that gets in her way of saying what she wants to say to a coworker. For example, you have a coworker who drives you crazy by calling you "dear," "hon," and "sweetie." You know his intentions are good. You know that he doesn't in any way mean to make you uncomfortable or to be patronizing, but you still don't like it. You haven't said anything because you keep telling yourself that you'll hurt his feelings. "I should have told him before. I'll really make him feel bad if he knows that it has bothered me for three years. I can't do that to him. I'll be embarrassed too. I can't do it now. I just will have to keep on acting like it doesn't bother me."

As long as that kind of internal speech goes on, you won't say a thing, even if your stomach is in a knot! But you can reframe your thinking about the problem and realize that "I'm doing John a favor by telling him that calling me dear makes me uncomfortable. Someone else who doesn't know him well may not realize his motives are good and may report him for sexual harassment. I'm protecting him, not hurting him, by being open and direct with him."

Reframing your thinking as a way to decrease the barriers to good communication can also be effective if you're mentally blaming someone. "He's a jerk and he deserves to get nailed for saying what he did." That kind of negative internal thinking often results in an aggressive outburst that you regret. A way to reframe your internal conversation is to say to yourself, "His intentions are OK. I have no reason to think he has bad motives." Finally, if your internal monologue tends toward the "Why bother?" type, you can also use reframing to change your thinking. Generally, "Why bother?" negative thinkers don't say much under any circumstances because they don't think anything will change. By reframing the entire aim of speaking up—to feel good about yourself instead of to change other people—you can be motivated to change your communication pattern.

Challenge

Challenging the negative thinking, another way to alter your internal dialogue, often works well for me. I ask myself, "What's the worst thing that could possibly happen if I do what I want to do but am afraid to do?" Then I ask, "Can I handle that outcome? How?"

If I'm concerned that being direct and telling someone what I want will result in their telling me that I can't have what I want, I guess that's the worst thing that can possibly happen. I try to catastrophize and exaggerate the outcome. They'll tell me that I shouldn't ask for what I'm asking for. They'll tell me that my directness is offensive and out of step with the context of the relationship. They'll tell me absolutely, positively no. Then I decide whether I can or can't handle that kind of outcome and if I can, how. I decide what I might say in the worst case scenario: how I might feel, how I can handle the conversation with the target person, as well as how I can handle my feelings afterward with myself. Once I think about it, the worse isn't so terrible, and even if it is, once I figure out how I can handle it I feel pretty relaxed about it. You can too.

Stop

If you're truly an obsessive negative thinker, trying to challenge or cognitively restructure your internal monologue just might get you deeper in the hole. If using coping statements and reframing confuses the issues—now you've got an internal dialogue instead of a monologue with warring factions making action even harder to take—then you need to learn the Stop technique. It's really a behavior modification technique that comes simply from pairing the negative thinking with an almost reflexive Stop picture or auditory word in your head. Sometimes I ask class participants to say their now habitual negative thinking out loud and as they get deeply into their internal monologue, I yell, "Stop." I interrupt them, scare the heck out of them, and give them a reminder of the Stop technique that they're unlikely to forget.

You can get a friend to do the same thing, or you can do it yourself. You can tape record the Stop or you can just quietly interrupt your internal negative ramblings with a loud external self-Stop yell. You can also use a visual image of a Stop sign or a policeman's hand, white-gloved, holding up traffic and in your face.

A slight change of tactics to accomplish the same stopping of the negative thinking relies on a rubber band. Place the rubber band around your wrist. When you catch yourself immersed in the negative thinking, start snapping the rubber band on your wrist. It stings! Snapping the rubber band serves as an undesirable consequence of the negative thinking. It's also a good metaphor. What you're doing to your wrist with the rubber band, you're also doing to your brain with your negative thinking— producing pain.

Visual Imagery

Mental images other than the stop images also can blow away the negative thinking. You can imagine erasing it or turning the volume down on it, as if your mind were a radio. You can send the negative thoughts away in the basket of a hot air balloon or put them in a garbage bag and haul them off to the dump. Any of these approaches can clear your mind of the mental barrier that is getting in your way. Having an empty mind is better any day than having a mind full of negative monologue: You can fill the empty with good neutral instructions.

4

Making a Plan, Picking a Technique

Once you've eliminated the barriers to good communication, or at least temporarily removed them, you're ready to pick a technique that will accomplish your chosen goal. In this chapter I describe a variety of communication characteristics and techniques that you can use to achieve your aims.

The various assertive techniques are so complete that you would never need to use any other communication form. Admittedly, you might feel limited and even somewhat bored with your own range of conversational variety, but you could use only assertive techniques and be an excellent communicator. Sometimes people enjoy using communication tacks like sarcasm, put-downs, metaphors, or humor. Although these approaches don't fit the mold of assertive communication, they may accomplish exactly what's wanted in a conversation. The departures from assertiveness may add a lot of desirable spice and interest to communication, as well as potential conflict. Your task is to pick and implement the technique that will work most effectively to accomplish your specific goal.

You want to be able to pick a technique rather than to be caught off guard and communicate impulsively or be ineffectively quiet. You want to be in the position of choosing what's going to work best for you in any given situation. When you don't feel in control, you revert to old habits. Instead of actively deciding how to do what you want, you may just let a situation happen. Then you let a problem stay a problem instead of translating it into a goal and taking action!

Brief and Specific

The communication characteristic that single-handedly can add the most to your competency as a communicator is being Brief and Specific. When you plan a conversation that relies on brevity and specificity, you'll immediately feel more comfortable knowing you only have to work on two or three consecutive comments. You don't have to, and shouldn't, plan and present a soliloquy. Many people think that the greater the volume of talk, the more the details, the more convincing they are to others. Not true.

When you're Brief and Specific, other people are more likely to hear what you say, to understand what you say, and to take you seriously. When you're concise, you avoid giving the other communicator extraneous information that they can use to argue against you. Thinking and communicating clearly helps the other person think and respond clearly, and, hopefully, concisely as well.

A senior level manager I work with as a consultant is extremely intelligent: He's a true visionary, a creative, flexible thinker, and a lengthy, imprecise talker. What happens? He loses his audience even though he has great messages to deliver. He loses them with rambling, with repetition, and with vagueness. As he works on his communication he sees better results. Recently, he commented that every day that goes by he recognizes more surely that good communication is always brief communication.

Eliminate Disclaimers, Apologies

Women in particular often are overly apologetic and explanatory in their speech. "I'm sorry to bother you with this, and perhaps I should have figured this out myself, but I've only been in the job a few weeks and. . . ." When you eliminate the preliminary excess, you can quickly get to the point. Briefly and specifically, you can say, "I need five minutes of help with the fax machine."

Reduce Unnecessary Details and Explanations

Cut to the chase, get to the point, say what needs to be said are all ways of saying start at the end rather than the beginning. When you're giving instructions, answering a question, or telling about a project, rather than starting with the history or talking about the building blocks or pieces, have the first sentence or paragraph tell it all. "I'd like you to assemble a team this week to work on improved report generation." Certainly you'll add details, answer questions, but to start with, state the end point briefly and specifically. The alternative, which is more common but less desirable because it's less clear, is, "I know you have a lot on your plate right now, but there's a huge increase in the number of complaints about reports. All different departments are frustrated with the fact that we don't get them out on time, and they don't seem to contain the right information for each individual department. Everyone wants more customization than they used to want. I don't know if we can generate that kind of report with our new system or not, but we should give it a try. Would you consider putting a team together this week to start working on the problem?"

Make Statements, Don't Ask Questions

For people who have trouble speaking up, learning to tell instead of ask is a good way to begin to sound and feel more assertive. I'm not suggesting that you never ask a question, but you should increase the frequency of delivering your message in statement form. A common type of question that nonassertive people may ask in a group situation is, "Don't you think that it might be better if we met on Friday instead of Monday?" What they mean is, "I think it would be better if we met on Friday instead of Monday." The statement form is clearer and avoids the possibility that others may just respond with, "No, I don't." Then you're in an awkward spot. You could still say, "Well, I'd actually prefer to meet Friday rather than Monday," but it would be anticlimactic after you'd first asked others for their opinion and had been told clearly that they didn't want to meet Friday.

Often people ask questions rather than make statements as a hedge against disagreement or argument. Let's say Jordan doesn't think the project team members are moving as fast as they should to get the project done by the deadline. He's worried that if he says, "I'm concerned. Unless we pick up the pace, we're going to miss the deadline for completion of the project," his teammates will respond negatively, for example, "Jordan, you're too uptight. We'll get it done. Chill out." Or, "Sounds like you don't have faith in your team, Jordan. That's not being a good team player." So instead of making a statement, Jordan asks a question. "Do you think we're going to get this done on time?" To which most people will respond, "Sure." Possibly some team members may read the "real" message behind the question and give him the same kind of response he feared getting if he made a statement. "I'm not worried, but it sounds like you are, Jordan. Sounds like you've lost the faith." It is better for Jordan to make the direct comment. State thoughts or beliefs and feelings directly. If someone disagrees with you, whether it's a colleague, boss, or someone who reports to you, at least the issue is out in the open and you can begin to do some problem solving. Otherwise the real concerns stay under the table, causing untold confusion and stress because no one knows what's really going on or who thinks what about the issues!

Many other types of question leave you in a powerless position:

"Does anybody else want to have this meeting off-site?"
"Do you think this is a good plan?"
"Are you ready to move into the next stage of the process?"

Saying instead, "I'd like to have the meeting planned as an off-site," sounds assertive and confident. "I think we need to revise the plan and provide more details." "I think we're ready to move into the next stage of the problem-solving process." These are all ways to translate the question into a statement and deliver your message more effectively.

For people who tend to be aggressive, the use of statements rather than questions to deliver the message can decrease the intimidation that other people may feel talking with you. A barrage of questions can seem like an interrogation, even if your intention is only to gather information.

"Who told you to do it like that?"
"What's the point of wasting your time doing something so repetitive?"
"Why would you think I would agree with that assignment?"
"How did you come to that conclusion?"

If your goal is to intimidate your coworker or subordinate, then the interrogation approach may work. If you want to deliver the message in a way that increases the likelihood that the listener will hear and understand you and not get defensive, making a statement works better.

> "I'm wondering who gave you the instructions that you followed to complete the report."
> "It doesn't seem efficient for you to be doing that repetitive work."
> "I get the impression that you thought I had agreed to have you carry out this assignment."
> "I'd like to understand more about how you came to that conclusion."

For both the nonassertive and the aggressive person, a decrease in question asking and an increase in statement making is useful. Certainly question asking is essential at times, but get in the habit of thinking whether the question or statement form is more useful in a given situation with a specific target person.

Eliminate the "Why" Question Altogether

The "why" question always puts people on the defensive and almost never gets you what you want, unless what you want is to punish the target person and bulldoze them.

> "Why were you late?"
> "Why did you plan the meeting from 9 to 5?"
> "Why didn't you send those notices out last week?"
> "Why are you so uptight about the deadline?"

Those questions all imply criticism, advice giving, or moralizing, for example:

> "You shouldn't have been late."
> "It was a mistake to plan the meeting from 9 to 5."
> "Those notices went out late and it's your fault."
> "You should hang loose."

Even if the asker of the "why" question doesn't have bad motives, the message receiver or target person is going to feel defensive. The defensiveness is almost a learned response for many of us, resulting from patterns of behavior we learned as a child. Generally, parents don't say to kids, "Why did you get such good grades this semester?" "Why are you and your brother playing so well without fighting?" "Why is your room so clean?" Instead they say, "Why are your grades so bad?" "Why do you and your brother always fight?" and "Why are you such a slob?" This experience crosses many cultures and is readily identified by a broad spectrum of grown-ups. That's why responding defensively to the "why" question is almost a reflex!

There are many ways, other than the "why" question, to get the information and answers that you want. You can ask, "How come?" Or instead of saying, "Why did you plan the meeting from 9 to 5?" you can say, "I'd rather the meeting start at 8:30 and end at 3:30 to avoid end of the day traffic." Making a statement rather than asking a question often works well and the person doesn't feel as defensive.

If you must know the answer to the "why" question, that is, you really need to know someone's intrinsic motivation, asking another kind of question is still preferable to asking "why?" For example, "What factors did you consider in deciding to hold the meeting from 9 to 5?" Or you can still make a statement to get at motivation or decision making. "I'd like to understand what determined your decision to meet from 9 to 5." The person may still feel criticized, but won't be quite as guarded or defensive as with the "why" question.

"I" Statements

While we're talking about questions and statements, let's address the specific "I" statement. The "I" statement is simply a sentence that begins with "I."

"I don't agree with you."
"I am concerned about your performance."

"I'm pleased that you've been improving your customer service process."
"I want all supervisors to make the prevention of sexual harassment their number one focus."

The purposes of the "I" statement are to avoid other communication habits that don't work well and to take ownership and
possession of the statement. By using "I," you avoid being vague
and general. For example, "Some people might not see things
the same way you do," is a general and not accountable way of
saying, "I don't agree with you." An equally ineffective alternative that you avoid by using "I" is to come across as aggressive
and hostile. "You don't know what you're talking about." By
saying again, "I don't agree with you," you've delivered a very
clear message that's not threatening and that shows your ownership of the opinion, thought, belief, or action.

Telling What You Want

Telling What You Want is an extension of the "I" statement. It
has three parts: I feel _____ when you _____ and I
want _____. The opening "I feel" segment of the statement is
completed by the addition of a word that expresses an emotion:
enthusiastic, uptight, angry, worried, concerned, pleased, satisfied. Expressing a feeling accomplishes two objectives: It gives
the listener information about yourself that helps them understand the impact of their behavior or the situation on you, and,
by stating a feeling rather than an opinion, you avoid putting
yourself into an argumentative situation. A feeling is really not
arguable. No one can tell you that you don't feel the way you
say you feel. They can tell you that you shouldn't feel that way,
or that they wouldn't feel that way, but they can't tell you you're
wrong in the way they could if you expressed an opinion.

Here's the difference in expressing a feeling and expressing
an opinion. "I feel concerned (or I'm concerned) when you don't
return my calls and I'd like you to get back to me within twenty-
four hours," expresses a feeling, concern. "I feel that you're
avoiding me when you don't return my calls and I'd like you to

get back to me within twenty-four hours," expresses an opinion, that you're avoiding me. When "that" appears after "feel," you can be sure that a belief or opinion follows. In the latter situation, you can go off on a tangent discussing whether the target person is or is not avoiding you and whether your opinion is or is not correct. The tangent keeps you from dealing with the important issue, which is that you want the person to return your call within twenty-four hours. In the former situation, the target person can say, "You should chill out. Don't be concerned." You don't have to go off on a tangent, but can just see Fogging and Broken Record (see those topics) and respond, "Perhaps I could worry less about the issue, but I do want my calls returned within a day." The emphasis stays where it needs to stay, on the change or improvement you want.

The second part of the Telling What You Want technique calls for you as the speaker to specifically describe, rather than label, the behavior or the situation that you are having positive or negative feelings about. Some examples of describing rather than labeling are:

"I feel uncomfortable when you hug me in a business setting."
"I'm pleased that the presentations to the board of directors were so clear, brief, and quantitative."
"I'm disappointed that your presentation didn't include statistical support."

Labeling, rather than describing, would sound like this:

"I feel uncomfortable when you act inappropriately."
"I'm pleased by your professionalism."
"I'm disappointed with your presentation style."

The third and essential part of the Telling What You Want technique is stating exactly what you want. There are a variety of ways to do that: "I'd like," "I want," "I prefer," "I'd suggest," "I demand," "I'd rather," "I'd choose to." The total three-part communication could sound like this: "I feel uncomfortable when you hug me in a business setting and I'd prefer to shake hands." Or, "I'm disappointed that your presentation didn't include statistical support. I'd like a hard copy of the quantitative data you collected as measures of outcome."

The Telling What You Want technique has broad applicability in the business setting. Men and women both can add it to improve their repertoire of communication skills. Women have a tendency to be very good at expressing their feelings and describing the situation or behavior that they are encountering, particularly when it's something they don't like. They're not as good at stating clearly and openly what they want. On the other hand, men are good at stating what they want, but often leave out the feeling words. Using all three parts is necessary for the effectiveness of the technique.

Broken Record

Repeating in a slightly different way what you have already said is a good way to stay firm and stick with your point. You avoid going off on a tangent or sounding pigheaded. Imagine you're in a discussion with a small team working on transferring people from one geographic location to another. Your opinion is that people should have a choice about the transfer. If they choose to stay where they are, that's OK, although they won't get the promotion they would get if they transferred. An alternative position held by several people is that if people choose not to take the promotion and transfer offered, they should be laid off. Here are some different ways you can restate your position using Broken Record after your initial presentation of your opinion:

> "I think our employees should have a choice about leaving or staying, without the threat of termination as a factor."
> "In my opinion, forcing people to transfer doesn't fit with our culture change."
> "In my experience, it's better not to give people the impression that they have a choice if in fact the consequences of one choice is being laid off."

Saying "No"

There is not one right way to say "no," but there are plenty of wrong ways. For example, "I'd love to, but I can't." "I wish I could, but the dog is sick, my mother-in-law is coming to visit, I have a project due that Monday, and I'm really not feeling well," are ways not to say it.

The bare-bones way—the simplest, shortest, and most certain for people who can't trust themselves to really say no—is to open the sentence with "No" followed by one brief reason. Then, follow that statement with Broken Record. A sequence would sound like this: Mike asks you to come in to work for a couple of hours early Saturday morning. You really don't want to do that and don't think you have to or need to. You tell Mike, "No. I don't want to do that this weekend." When he continues to push you, you use Broken Record. "It just doesn't work for me." "It won't be possible."

In one way, this approach is simple for people who are saying no because they don't have to remember a lot. In another way, it's difficult because people prefer to give excuses, apologies, and softeners. They seem to feel less guilty with the excuses approach. The bare-bones approach I'm suggesting seems tough, but it works and it saves getting into a long persuasion. If you need to soften the no, then you can always add a sentence:

"Please ask me again another time."
"Maybe tomorrow would work better for me."
"I'd like to be able to help you with that another time."

Fogging

Fogging is a technique that originated with Manual J. "Pete" Smith, who wrote a book called *When I Say No, I Feel Guilty.* (An excellent workplace training film has been developed from the book, which emphasizes a variety of communication techniques, the two most valuable of which are fogging and negative inquiry.) Fogging as a technique is particularly useful for dealing with criticism. You respond as if you were a fog bank: persistent, offering no resistance to penetration, not fighting back. He uses other phrases to describe the technique: agreeing with truth, agreeing in principle, agreeing with the odds. On first impression Fogging doesn't seem very assertive: It sounds like a cop-out. To Fog someone means to admit that there might be some truth to what they are saying, about you in particular. Your goal is to stop the direction and focus of the conversation.

Suppose your boss says, "You need to think more strategically and less operationally." You know that she has long held that opinion about you. You've discussed her concern before. From your viewpoint you are making progress on being more strategic, but you don't want to get defensive or get into a discussion about the topic now. So you say, "I certainly could be a better strategic thinker than I am." That's it. You don't say you will. You don't say you're working on it or making progress. You don't promise outcomes. You just acknowledge that there might be some truth in what she says. Generally, Fogging effectively discontinues the topic of conversation because there's not much that your boss can say other than, "Well, good. I'm glad you recognize that."

Certainly you wouldn't want to use Fogging if you perceived yourself as selling your soul. For example, if your boss said to you, "Martha, you're the worst supervisor I've ever seen," you're not going to say, "You know, I probably am a pretty poor supervisor." That would be selling your soul. But most of the time when someone is critical of us, there is some truth to it. We're not selling our souls to recognize and acknowledge that truth rather than reacting automatically and defensively. When you Fog, you can also state the response in a positive, rather than a negative, way. For example, in response to "You never listen well to instructions," you could Fog with, "I'm not a very good listener," or "I could be more attentive." The latter sounds more upbeat and positive than the former, even though both are examples of Fogging.

Negative Inquiry

Negative Inquiry is similar to Fogging because they are both ways to deal with criticism in a nondefensive manner. Negative

Inquiry is a questioning form. When someone criticizes you, you ask them for more information as a way to avoid the automatic defensive response as well as to avoid being manipulated by someone effectively hitting your hot button.

Using the same example as mentioned under Fogging, your boss tells you that you need to start thinking more strategically and less operationally. A Negative Inquiry would be, "What is it about my operational thinking that is problematic?" Or, "What has happened that leads you to conclude I'm not think-ing strategically?" Or, "How has my operational rather than strategic thinking been a barrier?" These questions give you more information about the other person's concern and avoid the knee-jerk justification or defensiveness, that elicit more criti-cism and a self-defeating pattern.

Putting It Together

Most of the techniques described are used in combination with each other, or with listening responses, rather than as one single response to a statement to you from a speaker. Certain tech-niques will become easier for you to use than others and you'll prefer some to others. Some situations will almost automatically elicit certain techniques. If someone does something that really bugs you, Telling What You Want is a natural.

It doesn't matter if you use all the techniques all the time. What matters is that you broaden your repertoire of communi-cation skills and feel comfortable that you can choose how to communicate in a broad variety of circumstances.

5
Saying No and Meaning It

The Situation

Saying "no" to people who ask you to do things that you don't want to do, and don't have to do, can be extremely difficult. The inability to say "no," the fears associated with saying "no," and the consequences of saying "yes" when you really mean "no" have been cited as major factors in time management problems as well as a contributing cause of psychosomatic illness.

A 1995 nationwide survey of 1,000 sexually active girls sixteen years old and younger, was described by Judith Mann, a *Washington Post* columnist. It identified these adolescent respondents' perceived need for more information related to sex and sexuality. The major concern of these young women was knowing how to say "no" without hurting the other person's feelings. Although the population is youthful and the focus not business related, the respondents' inability to say "no" to sex, even though they may have feared pregnancy or disease, demonstrates the even more powerful fear of rejection. The findings also illuminate the continuing need for assertive communication skills.

In a newspaper column on business, Dale Dauten notes that "no" may be the most underutilized business tool available. He comments that business people hear so much about being positive and optimistic that they can easily forget the important role of saying "no" for setting clear limits and boundaries. Whether in personal or in work situations, men and women are very concerned about other people's reaction to their "no."

Will the other person think you are rude, insensitive, uncaring?

Will they retaliate by not helping you out when you're in need?

Will they never ask you to do anything for them or with them again?

Will they reject you from that "no" point on?

A kindly colleague of mine, Joe, works with a young woman who always wanted him to go out to lunch with her. She wanted to get to know him better, to improve their working relationship, and to pick his brain because he is more experienced than she. Joe didn't want lunch out to be a part of their working relationship for a variety of reasons. His philosophy of marriage, and he is married, precludes socializing alone with female colleagues. The young woman, Annette, argued with Joe when he tried to explain his viewpoint. She told him that he is discriminating against her because he does have lunch with male colleagues. Joe was more than willing to give her some mentoring or coaching at their place of business, but not over breakfast, lunch, or dinner off the work site. The ongoing conflict was annoying Joe. The sore subject was also beginning to set the theme for the entire working relationship between Joe and Annette. Finally, Joe, with some help from me, was able to initiate this "no": "Annette, I don't want to go out to lunch with you. I know you would like to do that, but I wouldn't. There's no reason that I have to do that, and I'm not going to. I've said everything I have to say on the subject. I really don't want it brought up any more. It's a dead issue, a done deal."

Her response? "OK. I understand." Previously, his feeling of guilt kept Joe from sounding firm and final, so Annette kept pushing the issue. This time, he said what he meant, he meant what he said, and Annette heard his message loud and clear. The issue wasn't brought up again, and their relationship improved dramatically.

Saying "no" isn't necessarily limited to being a responder in a conversation when you've been asked to do something that you don't want to do. Saying "no" can also be presented as an initiation by you as the speaker. Let's say your boss has started asking you to stay overtime several times a week during the last month. You don't want this to turn into a regular, expected behavior from you. Rather than waiting for the next time he asks, you might initiate the topic. "I've decided that I'm not going to work overtime more than once during the week from now on. My workout is so essential to my stress management plan that I can't afford to give it up more than one day a week. If there's extra work to be done, I'll figure out another time to do it rather than after 5."

When you take the initiative in telling the person up front the "no," you save yourself from being caught off guard with

their request. You can time the comment best, and you are probably in more control of yourself and the situation. You fend off
the requests, at least for a while.

Once the courage to actually say "no" is acquired, many
people are pleasantly surprised at how well accepted their "no"
is. Whether they do it as the initiator or the responder, particularly when they sound as if they mean what they say, their point
of view is respected.

A different variation of the same theme came from Terissa,
a participant in a recent assertive communication class that my
husband and I taught. Her boss kept wanting her to do more
work, extra work, other people's work, and his work. Terissa
had a terrible time saying "no." She would stumble over her
words, feel guilty and apologize, be fearful that she might be
fired. She usually ended up doing the extra work, even when
she was doing somebody else's unfinished work, and even
when she had to come in on the weekend. Finally, she found
a way to say "no" that was comfortable for her. She never
really used the word "no," but she made herself very clear.

One day her boss came in and said, "I really need those
papers related to the Sherwood case taken care of today." Terissa said, "Gwen and I have talked and she will be taking care
of that case." He responded with an "OK," but was back in an
hour with a repeat request. "This case is top priority and I really
want you to take care of it for me. It's imperative that it's done
today and done well."

Using a version of the Broken Record technique Terissa
responded, "I just checked with Gwen and she understands
this is high priority." Again he answered, "OK." Within an hour
Terissa's boss was back saying, "I want you to take care of this
Sherwood thing and get it done now. You're the only one who
really understands the whole picture." One more time, calmly
and in a quiet, firm voice, Terissa said, "It's being taken care of
by Gwen as we speak."

Terissa never said the dreaded (to her) word "no" to her
boss, but she continued to communicate very clearly to him
that she was not going to do what he asked her to do, what she
didn't want to do, really didn't have to do, and even shouldn't

have had to do. How was she able to be so assertive with him? His requests were made during her last week of work. She had decided to leave her job because she was so stressed by the pressure she felt at her boss's demands and her own inability to be assertive. She decided to leave because she saw no other option.

Now, knowing that being fired wasn't a possibility, since she had already resigned, she felt confident in being assertive. And it worked. The essential factor in allowing Terissa to alter her behavior and effectively use the Broken Record technique was her altered thinking. When she was anticipating a continuing relationship she thought to herself, "I can't say no. I have to do whatever he asks me to do, or he'll think I'm incompetent and maybe fire me." Now that she had resigned, she was able instead to say to herself, "I have nothing to lose by sticking to my guns and saying what I want to say."

If she had been able to say "no" to her boss when she was overwhelmed, when he was delegating too much work to her, or when he was asking for too much overtime, she would not have ended up in the position of feeling she had to resign to survive! The situation could have been a successful experience for Terissa and her boss. She could have stayed, doing the kind of work that she basically enjoyed and was good at. She could have avoided looking for another job. Her boss wouldn't be in the position of losing a valuable employee. He also would have saved the time and money involved in hiring and training a new employee.

The consequences of saying "yes" when you really want to say "no," or of saying "no" but ultimately behaving "yes," can be devastating and long-term. You teach people that you don't mean what you say, which puts them in the position of having to second-guess you all the time ("Are you sure you really don't mind staying late?") or of manipulating you because they know that you're an easy target for guilt induction ("I really hate to ask you because I know that your workout after work is top priority for you, but could you just consider this one time putting work in first place and staying late on Wednesday?").

The IMB MO for Saying "No"

How do you get to the point where you can say "no," or variations on the theme of no, when you need to say it, with whom
you need to say it, and feel comfortable saying it? Going back to
the IMB MO, discussed in Chapter 2, the first place to start is
identifying what you want. You have to be able to say to yourself, if to no one else to start with, "I really don't want to do
this," or "I really do want to do this," and then decide how you
want to convey the message. The first and second questions you
ask yourself in any situation that is causing you some discomfort
are "What do I want?" and "What's best for me?" In the situation just described, Terissa had no trouble deciding that she
wanted to not work so much overtime and to not do work that
other people could and should be doing. She wanted to do her
assigned work in a regular work day and not be burdened with
other assignments, because she was a fast and dependable
worker.

Identify the Negative Thinking

Often people don't allow themselves to decide what they want
because they overcrowd their mind with such thoughts as:

"I should want to"
"It's my job so what I want doesn't matter"
"I can't do anything about it anyway so what difference does
    it make what I want?"

Once you have the negative thoughts related to saying "no"
clearly in mind, you can continue in the IMB MO and make
further adjustments and adaptations and perhaps at some time
even ask yourself the questions, "What does he or she want?"
and "What's best for them?" Usually nonassertive people think
of the other person and never think about themselves, so they
not only don't know what they want, but they most certainly
don't get it except by a random stroke of luck! And then they
can't give themselves credit for it.

The negative thinking that gets in potential "no" sayers' way is wrapped up with fears of hurting other people's feelings, fears of retaliation and rejection, fears of being disliked or being seen as unfriendly or uncooperative in the workplace, and even of being fired. Difficulty saying "no" is primarily the problem of the "I'm not good enough," nonassertive person rather than the "Why bother?" or the "You're not OK" person! Frequent internal monologues go like this:

> "He'll think I'm not a good team player if I don't say yes, particularly if everyone else does."
> "She'll think I'm mean if I don't help her out with her overload."
> "They'll think I'm unfriendly if I don't go out to lunch with them."

Substitute, Challenge, and Stop

When you have difficulty saying "no," cognitive restructuring of the internal dialogue to help you say what you want to say is the place to start. Some possibilities are:

> "I have the right to say no."
> "If I say 'yes' instead of 'no' I'll feel worse than if I say 'no.'
> "Saying 'no' is taking good care of myself."
> "I can always offer to help later if I say 'no' now. If I say 'yes' now, I'm stuck!

If you decide to challenge your negative thinking, then ask yourself, "What's the worst that can possibly happen?" Realistically speaking, the worst that can possibly happen is that the other person is disappointed in or angry at you. How can you handle that? You can remind yourself that they will recover from their disappointment, hurt, or irritation. You will have other opportunities, at your initiation or theirs, to be supportive, helpful, or attentive. If they are the kind of person who's going to hang on for life to their anger at you, then sooner or later you would have lost the relationship. Or you would have allowed yourself to be held hostage by them and your fear of rejection.

You could also reframe the situation. When you say "yes" to someone when you want to say "no," you're avoiding hurting their feelings, but you're hurting yourself. Eventually the built-up resentment of continually complying, agreeing, going along with someone else's wants and needs at the expense of your own, can cause physical and psychological problems. The resentment, verbalized or not, will also ultimately interfere with the relationship between you and the other person. Saying "no," reframed, becomes a way to take good care of yourself and to do the other person a favor, by preventing future deterioration of the relationship.

A final suggestion for dealing with the negative thinking is to reframe a "no" by becoming desensitized to it. When saying "no" is a source of fear and angst, the word takes on gigantic proportions in your mind. Saying "no" out loud to yourself in the shower, or in the car, yelling it, whispering it, saying it crisply, saying it in an elongated N-o-o-o form, saying it with warmth or with hostility, helps to return the word to its rightful proportions. It's just a word like "hot" or "cold," "up" or "down," and saying it, softly or loudly, has no built-in frightening consequences.

Select a Technique

The Assertive "No" Response

The assertive responder is the person who is asked to do something for someone else, or to do something that isn't her job, or to do someone a favor, or to do anything that she doesn't want to do and doesn't have to do, who is able to respond positively, honestly, and directly and say "No." There are a variety of different ways to accomplish this task. For the weak at heart, I'll start with the "softest" way and then move along the continuum to the tougher ways to deliver this no message in a way that people can receive it.

If saying "no" is difficult, find another way to say "no," and add one and only one reason. Pick an easy situation and a person you are comfortable with. When a coworker asks you to go out of the building for lunch and you can't afford the time, you say, "I can't go today. I have too much work to finish this afternoon." Then you use Broken Record if he keeps pushing you.

"Not today. I'm going to stay at my desk."
"I'm not going to take time for lunch today."
"I'll grab something later."

The next step up in saying "no" assertively is to be sure that "no" is the first word in the first sentence out of your mouth. A good direct approach, with a little softener thrown in, sounds like this. "No, Mark, I can't stay late tonight. I know you need help and I guarantee my full attention and energy tomorrow, but I just can't do it tonight. I have play tickets and I'm going with a group." When you don't start out with "no," a long, wandering sentence that never states clearly what you mean may come out, for example, "I'd really like to help out tonight, but I have stayed late a lot this week and there are other people who haven't put in as much time as I have who you never seem to ask and maybe it would be better to ask them but if you really can't get anyone else to work and you're desperate I suppose I could stay an extra hour or two, but it doesn't really seem fair." In response you may well end up with, "Great. I really appreciate your willingness to stay." This comment leaves you without an option. Or you start again sounding and feeling like a whiner, moaner, and complainer rather than like a person who is standing up for her rights.

What's the worst that can possibly happen? Your boss can order you to stay, which is unlikely. In that case, you can say, "It sounds like you're ordering me to stay late tonight," so he has a chance to rethink and recoup and recant if he wants to. If he doesn't and instead says, "That's exactly what I'm doing. You have no choice," then you can go in a variety of directions. You can be compliant and stay and tell him that you really don't like being ordered to stay late and you don't want it to happen again. You can still refuse to stay and tell him that as far as you know, staying overtime is not something he can order you to do and you are going to leave although you would be willing to stay late or come in early another time this week.

The boss could also use guilt induction techniques such as, "Well, it's my son's Little League game tonight and I'm missing it to work late. The least you can do is miss the play with your friends." Again, you can simply but straightforwardly use a Broken Record technique, making the same basic response in a slightly different way. "I'm sorry you're not going to be able to go to the game. I do need to meet my friends for the play tonight and I won't be able to stay any longer. I'd be happy to help you later this week." Then head out. Don't hang around for further discussion, persuasion, or guilt induction. Act like you mean what you say, which is to walk slowly and confidently toward the door!

The key is to respond initially to the request with a "no" as the first word in the sentence, followed by one reason, and if you really want to, a softener such as "I'm sorry," "I will be able to work later in the week," or "Another day would work better for me." Then whatever happens from that point on, you just use Broken Record to say the same thing over and over in a slightly different way, but without bending, unless you decide you want to bend.

Although it may seem paradoxical, once you're experienced and know that you can count on yourself to say "no" and stick with the "no," then you can eliminate "no" from the very beginning of your sentence. The real purpose of that first clearly stated "no" is to be sure that you want "no," mean "no," and say it. When you're confident in your ability to mean no, then you can start with, "I won't be able to stay late tonight. I've made plans that aren't changeable." You can always say "no" second or third round if needed. For example, if you get some flack from your boss, you can use Broken Record with "no." "No, Jack. It just isn't workable tonight."

If you're ready to escalate the firmness of the response to the request, then you can move into a more bare-bones approach. You still start out with the first word "no," but then you don't give an excuse, nor do you add a softener. You might say, "No, Jack. That won't work tonight." You still follow up any further presses, pushes, or threats by using Broken Record rather than offering excuses or softeners. So in response to a "Well, why not?" instead of giving a reason, you would say, in a Broken Record kind of way, "That's just not possible tonight," or "It just won't work out for tonight," or "There isn't a way I can make that happen." You may have to go on for a while with variations on the theme, but don't answer questions that will send you off on a tangent, make you become defensive or apologetic, or cause you to fold!

The Assertive No-as-Initiator

We tend to think of saying "no" primarily as a response for dealing with people who ask us to do things that we don't want to or don't have to do. But we can also say "no" to initiate a conversation, not just as a response. Obviously the technique is different. Here's a good example:

> Harry and Erin have been working together for about a year. Every month, before the staff meeting, Erin calls Harry and asks him to please bring the overhead projector from his office to the meeting. Every month Harry is annoyed to be asked to do this. He doesn't use the projector, he doesn't need it, often no one uses or needs it. He feels put upon to be always asked to bring it. He also thinks Erin is treating him like a valet instead of a coworker. It's no more his job than anyone else's to bring the projector to every meeting and he's annoyed that she always asks him to do it.
>
> Is this a big deal? No. But such small, nagging, and annoying situations can cause people to get tense and testy with each other unless they are dealt with. Harry could wait until Erin calls, and then tell her in response to her certain question, "No, Erin. I would like you to ask someone else to bring the projector for this week's meeting." But a variety of problems are inherent in that approach. Harry may be caught off guard with the timing of Erin's call and not be quite up to saying what he wants to say. The "no" response may feel more negative to the receiver than the "no" initiation.
>
> As the initiator, Harry can easily use an "I" statement as he's lugging the projector back to his office after this month's

meeting: "Erin. I would like you to get someone else to bring the projector next month. I think the responsibility could be shared among us all." This is the soft no-as-initiator.

If he wants the message to be firmer, Harry could use a stronger "I" statement, coupled with telling Erin what he'd like her to do. "I'm not going to bring the projector to the future staff meetings. I'd like you to call some other people to take responsibility for it." Or if he wants Erin specifically to know about his unhappiness with her, he could use the full Telling What You Want technique. "I would prefer that you not continue to call me to bring the projector to meetings. I'd like you to ask other people in the future."

Any of the responses are fine; it depends on what you want to accomplish as your outcome. If what you really want is to punish her for loading you down with this boring task for so long, then you could be aggressive. "I'm tired of being treated by you as if I'm your valet. I'm not and I don't want to be called again about bringing the overhead to our meetings. Get someone else to do it. Or carry it yourself!"

Remember

Being able to say no as the initiator or the responder is the first building block to being assertive. Once you've mastered the skill of no-saying, you'll have the confidence to move on to more complicated techniques. The techniques are not so difficult, but the ability to say "no" and to not necessarily give people what they want is key to continuing to be assertive in a nonhostile, constructive manner.

- The ability to say "no" as a responder or initiator is the essential number one building block of assertiveness. Stick with it until you get it. The rest will come more easily.
- "No" as the first word out of your mouth helps to ensure that you'll say what you want to say clearly when you're choosing to say you can't or don't want to do something.

- Give one brief reason, rather than multiple reasons, for the "no."
- As you get more skilled and confident, you can toughen or soften the "no" message.
- Taking the initiative to say "no" instead of waiting to say it as the response to a request can increase the likelihood that you'll do what you want to do in a way you want to do it.

6
Speaking Up and Speaking Out

The Situation

How many times have you, or someone you worked with, had a brilliant idea, mentioned it in a meeting, and had no response? Or, similarly, started to explain your great idea, been interrupted, and had someone else finish your thought and get the credit for the creative thinking? Or even worse, have you said something in a group or even in a one-to-one conversation and found that people just kept right on talking as if you hadn't said anything? After a few of these experiences, you may find that you don't say anything at all in work groups!

My running buddy, Harry, calls the no-response experience *denial of impact.* Most men and women have noticed a variation of the denial of impact experience in their work or personal situations. It can happen with one person; it can happen in a group. You can be, or feel, ignored at a formal meeting or at a casual social cafeteria lunch. It can happen for a variety of different reasons.

A common first denial of impact experience may occur during a meeting where you are in a position of lesser power in the group. Recently, a group of sixteen managers from different departments of a large corporation met to do some problem solving on common issues. The group had met several times previously and had developed some cohesiveness. A subgroup of ten members had met frequently before. They had been successful in taking on team roles, developing group norms, and solving some difficult problems unique to them. The total group began to talk about which one of several problems they were going to take on. Members appeared to be settling on a gigantic, long-standing problem in the marketing department, which many people thought was important because it affected everyone in the group.

One manager, Luis, a first-time attendee at this meeting, although not new to the group or the company, quietly mentioned to the group that he didn't think the problem affected him. Boom! He was leveled quickly by his boss, who firmly told him he just didn't understand if he thought the problem didn't affect him. Luis and his opinion were dismissed. The group moved on quickly, without giving Luis an opportunity to justify, defend, explain, or cry! They solidified their position that this was the best problem to discuss as a group. Luis said nothing for the next three hours.

A little later in the discussion another participant, Hoo, also new to this meeting and this group but not to the company, was brave enough to state his opinion. He wondered aloud if the Marketing problem was too big for this group to take on. Hoo suggested that maybe they should take on a smaller problem; a problem that they could solve quickly and easily and feel successful. Boom! Multiple voices rose to disagree with his thinking and tell him he didn't get it. Team members explained that this group solved big problems, not little problems, quickly and easily and felt successful. Hoo backed off quickly and quietly. He apologized, said it was just a thought, he was wrong, and he hadn't understood. He also didn't say a word for the rest of the day.

People like Luis and Hoo often are so devastated by the Boom that they shut down for a long time. The resulting fear of speaking up and speaking out can occur even when someone has previously been successful and confident in verbally contributing or presenting to a group.

The same shutdown can happen to a lesser degree when a group member says something and is ignored or is interrupted by someone expanding on his or her idea. The speaker often becomes less confident and says less or nothing next time. Then they're ignored until finally someone says, "Hey, Mary. What's the story? You never say anything in our meetings. You never speak up. It's part of your job to be a contributor, not to just sit there and listen or daydream. You're not being a good team player." A different kind of Boom! When that boom happens to you, you can be immobilized. While you're ignored, another attendee at the meeting can seem to ramble on about nothing and have everyone spellbound. No interruptions of him. No wandering gazes. No side conversations when he speaks. What's the deal?

My guess is the only differences between you and the rambler are that he has the power in the group, so people think they have to listen. Or he's more confident than you and acts as if he has the right to say what he thinks in an "I Mean Business" kind of way. When he acts that way, other people often respond positively. They respond as if he does mean what he says and he does know what he's talking about and he does have the right to say what he thinks. They reinforce his behavior, which makes him confident enough to keep on doing it.

In a recent survey I've been conducting about male-female communication in the workplace, one of the top three problems identified by several thousand men and women is "Women don't speak up." I know that many men have trouble speaking out and being heard as well, but the perception seems to be that women's lack of initiative is more of a problem than men's. In the competitive business culture of the nineties, both men and women need to be able to make their views and opinions known, directly, firmly, clearly, and briefly.

A recent *Wall Street Journal* article about the advantages and disadvantages of corporate managers taking overseas assignments mentioned the need to learn and be comfortable with indirect communication approaches when working in other countries. The article pointed out that the U.S. business culture primarily values directness. Consequently, managers returning to the United States, now expert in indirect communication, may be seen as wimps, poor team players, or noncontributors because they no longer speak up and speak out directly, another indication of the increasing demand for a broader, flexible, and adaptable repertoire of communication skills in today's global marketplace.

In any meeting you attend, you probably notice that the person who speaks up most is often viewed as knowledgeable and in control. These people usually speak up early in the meeting and continue to interject comments and opinions right up to the end. Unless they're ramblers, repeaters, or BSers, they are usually listened to. They acquire some status even if they don't have a high position relative to other members of the group.

The IMB Process for Speaking Up and Out

Using the good old reliable IMB MO to solve the communication problem again, start with Deciding What You Want. In most situations, although you don't speak up and out, you do want people to understand and know your viewpoint. Maybe you want to be more respected and valued in the work situation, and speaking up is a means to that end. Perhaps you want to be taken seriously in your work environment and speaking out is a means to that end.

Remembering about stating goals specifically, a possibility for setting the goal in this situation is: I want to state my opinion about the first topic that's brought up at the next staff meeting. This is a very clear and measurable want. You may have complex reasons for wanting to do this. You may hope to accomplish a variety of more abstract outcomes by doing it. It may be the first of a series of goals you're going to set to reach the desired end point; nonetheless it is clear and concise, and you'll know if you do it. Variations could be:

I want to state my opinion clearly and restate it in a different way if there's disagreement.

I want to stand up when I'm presenting information to a large group.

I want to speak more loudly and firmly and decisively when I'm making a report to a group.

I want to express my feelings as well as my thoughts about an issue, as an initiator of conversation or in response to a question.

I want to state my disagreement with an idea when I do disagree, even if the idea comes from my boss.

Identify the Negative Thinking

Whether you need to speak up as responder when someone is riding roughshod over your comments, or whether you're trying to get yourself to take the initiative in stating your opinions loudly and clearly and then continuing to back them up when someone disagrees, the negative thinking that serves as a barrier to doing it is often the same. Some very common thoughts of the "I'm not good enough" type are:

"They'll think I'm pushy if I say too much."
"He's the boss. He runs the meeting, not me."

"I'll just get run over more if I say anything."

"They're more experienced so my ideas probably don't have much value."

"No point in saying anything because they'll come back with a vengeance and then I won't know what to say next."

The internal monologue of most "I'm not good enough" thinkers is a huge barrier to speaking up and speaking out. They put their brain and mouth in Park with the negativity, yet expect movement. It just doesn't happen. Changing the negative thinking puts the brain and mouth in Drive so you can move forward and do what you want to do.

The "Why bother?" types among you may be saying to yourselves,

"What's the point? They never listen to me anyway."

"In the big picture, what I say doesn't matter."

"They'll just do what they want regardless."

Negative thinkers who tend toward the aggressive, "You're not good enough" type of internal monologue tend to say,

"I'm right so that gives me the right to interrupt and say what I think."

"I've got the solution already, so why waste time listening to everyone else?"

People with this kind of negative thinking don't have trouble speaking up or speaking out, but they do have trouble delivering their message in a way that it can be received. After a while, listeners to the aggressive speaking out communication turn off mentally and often show their annoyance nonverbally with sighs, eye rolls, slumping, or other behaviors.

Shelley Thompson, of The Don Jackson Company, uses the metaphor that if the ship misses the port, the fault doesn't lie with the port. In communication, aggressive speakers often miss the port because of their internal monologue.

Substitute, Challenge, and Stop

All three kinds of negative thinkers, the "I'm not good enough," the "Why bother?," and the "You're not good enough" communicators need to alter their negative thinking to a more neutral instructional monologue that moves them toward saying what they want to say so that people can receive their message. For all three types of thinkers, the same internal message could work: They would just come at it from different points along the continuum.

Starting with cognitive restructuring, here are some coping statements from the list that might work for you.

"As long as I keep my cool, I'm in control."
"Keep the focus on the present; what is it I want to do?"
"It's OK to make mistakes."

Some customized internal substitute statements are:

"I have the right to express my opinion."
"Not everyone will agree with me and that's OK."
"Speaking up may not make a big difference, but not speaking up gets me nowhere."
"Taking some communication risks is part of my job description."
"I'm going to be one of the first people to comment. I'll comment on a simple subject. That'll make it easier to speak up later on a tougher subject."

In addition to cognitive restructuring, maybe you need to challenge your negative thinking. What's the worst that could possibly happen? Someone could vehemently disagree with you after you've mustered your courage and very positively asserted your viewpoint. They could tell you that your idea is stupid. "Just keep your mouth shut if you don't have anything better to contribute," is a good worst case scenario comment. Unlikely, but possible.

If that happens, what could you say or do in response? How could you handle it? You could just say nothing. You could burst into tears and leave the room. You could say, "I don't appreciate having my comment called stupid." Regardless of what you do, you'll undoubtedly feel bad for an hour or two, but you won't get fired, you won't get into a knock-down confrontation, and you probably won't faint! Decide on a substitute, challenge, or stop approach that would work, tuck it away for future reference, and begin to think about what and how you're going to make your first stab at speaking up and out in situations that are tough for you.

Select a Technique

One way to move yourself into speaking up and speaking out at a meeting is to concentrate on saying something, anything, early on in a meeting. When you do that, you've already removed a barrier and you've already accomplished a goal. Speaking up early in a meeting also makes it easier to speak up later. Even if all you say is, "I agree," or "I had a different experience," or "Uh-huh," you've broken your own internal ice by speaking and hearing your voice. It works! Consider also the possibility of speaking louder, changing the tempo, changing chairs, or standing up, as ways of signaling that you're going to be participating in a different way.

Brief and Specific and "I" Statements

When you're speaking up in a difficult situation, the best techniques to use are the simplest. Being brief and specific will increase not only the likelihood that you can say what you want to say, but also the likelihood that you'll be heard. Eliminate the apologies and disclaimers, use few details, and start at the end instead of the beginning.

In the earlier situation with Luis, when his boss corrected him, he could have said simply and lightly, "I got it. I definitely want to work on this Marketing issue." A similar brief, slightly humorous approach could have been used by Hoo. "I clearly underestimated this group's capabilities." Here's an example of a wrong, but not unusual way to speak up in a meeting: "I know that most of you have much more experience than I do with this project, and as a matter of fact, more time with the company. But I've been thinking about it and actually doing some research on transfer policies within the company, historically I mean. You may say that this has been tried before, and maybe it has and I just didn't read about it, but I think we need to have different policies for people who want to transfer and for people who are being forced to transfer." The example is an exaggeration, but it makes the point!

Here's a right way, which is brief and specific and uses the "I" statement technique. You state simply what you think, or want, or feel, starting the statement with "I." "I think we need to have different policies for people who want to transfer and for people who are being forced to transfer." Be prepared to tell what you think those different policies should, could, or would be, but don't worry about defending your opinion, dealing with the "been there, done that" response, or explaining how and why you came to that conclusion. Keep the discussion forward moving, even if people try to throw up communication barriers. Regardless of what people might say, you don't have to respond directly to their comments, which may be going off on a tangent or may be putting you down. They may be ignoring what you said entirely!

After checking in to your internal monologue and substituting again ("I'm OK. I have a well-researched opinion here") your next comment might be, "When I discussed the issue briefly with Mark in Human Resources, he said he'd draw up a couple of sample policies for us to look at. I'll pass them out."

Other brief and specific "I" statements that you could make, depending on the situation, are:

"I wasn't finished talking. I'd like to continue."
"I don't agree."
"I have a very different experience than yours."
"I would like you to wait until I'm through before commenting. I'll be brief."

Broken Record

Another simple and useful technique that you can use is to repeat what you have already said, in a slightly different way, either with "I" statements or paraphrasing yourself.

"I think different policies would work."
"I think we need to change the transfer policy now."
"Similar policies for different situations isn't a good solution."
"The transfer issue has two separate components."

Telling What You Want

Another technique that you can use to firmly state what you want or think is best is the brief, specific, and clear Telling What You Want technique. Here's an example: "I feel confident that the forced and unforced transfers will be viewed very differently. I'd strongly suggest we have different policies for the different situations." Or a different adaptation of the same technique: "I'm certain that people see the forced and unforced transfer situations as completely different. Consequently, I'm in favor of having two separate policies."

Fogging

Fogging is a good way to be sure you say something, rather than crumbling in defeat if someone criticizes you. When your goal is to increase your confidence and visibility by speaking up more frequently, you need to be able to respond nondefensively to criticism. If you've finally ventured out on a limb to state an opinion, and your colleague tells you that he thinks your idea stinks, rather than keeping quiet, pushing back a little is more assertive. You could combine a fog with an "I" statement and say, "Maybe it's not a brilliant idea. I think we could use it as a seed for some brainstorming."

In the previous situation discussed, Luis could have used Fogging and said, "Maybe I should have seen that connection." Hoo might have Fogged with, "I could have given you more credit for problem-solving abilities." By saying something, rather than nothing, you keep yourself in the speaking-up arena.

Let's look at an entire conversation between you and several people who don't agree with you. In this conversation, you'll use only the techniques described previously.

> **You:**   "I think we need to start out dealing with the transfer issue and come up fairly quickly with

	two different policies: one for forced transfers and one for nonforced transfers."
Marla:	"I don't think you understand the transfer situation, Judy. You haven't been around as long as the rest of us and aren't familiar with the long history of conflict and competition that predates this discussion."
You:	"I may not be as acquainted with the history as those of you who have worked here longer. (Fogging) I do think I have a good grasp of the current situation."
Stan:	"There's a lot of overlap, which makes it a complex issue and not as simple as you may think."
You:	"I recognize the complexity of the problem. I think using the simplest solution possible is often a good way to start solving problems."
Sylvia:	"That's not right. If you have a complex problem, you have to have a complex solution. You're oversimplifying the situation."
You:	"Perhaps I am. I'd like to hear some of the ideas that you think would work."

The entire conversation on your part used only "I" statements and Fogging, being Brief and Specific. You never sounded defensive, argumentative, or stubborn, but you made your point. You then, graciously and with wisdom, moved the burden of proof to one of the dissenters, Sylvia, again without being resentful or defensive. Certainly, you can add other assertive communication techniques, but the dialogue demonstrates how simple speaking up and speaking out can be.

Remember

As long as you stay quiet, you become invisible. As long as you stay invisible, you have little impact and little chance for promotion, advancement, or the plum projects. You don't have to turn loud and obnoxious, but begin to get more comfortable and practiced at speaking up, speaking out, briefly and frequently.

- Start changing that negative thinking quickly. Start giving yourself good instructions.
- Be one of the first people to speak at a meeting and make it brief. It doesn't matter much what you say, but saying something releases your voice and increases the likelihood that you'll say something significant later.
- Use as few words as possible to say what you think. Being brief and specific, using "I" statements, increases the likelihood that you'll speak up because you know you don't have to talk for long.
- Check with friendly co-workers to see if you need to speak more loudly, or stand up, or use more variety in your voice patterns to grab the group's attention.

7

Telling It Like It Is

Giving your colleagues specific positive and negative information about their performance and the impact of their behavior
on you or the organization is an indispensable skill. With the
exception of the blaming aggressive person, most people dread
giving negative feedback to anyone under any circumstances.
Often, Telling It Like It Is dredges up catastrophic thinking on
the part of the deliverer of the message! What happens? The
message doesn't go out directly. Whether a situation involves
your boss, a coworker, or someone who reports to you, the best
thing to do is let people know early and clearly what you need
or want from them and what you can provide for them. If you
tell them what you expect and what to expect from you, there's
far less chance for future misunderstanding.

A graduate of the assertive communication class, whose experience as a nonassertive communicator with a demanding
boss resulted in her resigning from her job (see Chapter 5),
began her new job entirely differently. Terissa had learned! In
her second interview for the job, she communicated clearly that
she wanted a regular workday, from 9 to 5. She stated her willingness to occasionally stay late or come in on weekends for
special projects, but affirmed her strong desire to obtain a job
that didn't demand or expect frequent overtime.

Once Terissa was hired, she continued to be a clear, direct
communicator with her boss and coworkers. When her boss
asked her a somewhat personal question about her last job, she
assertively said, "I'd prefer not to talk about that." When Terissa's boss gave her an order, in a somewhat high-handed manner,
Terissa was startled and fell back into fears of autocratic bosses
leftover from the last job. She later told her boss, "I get very
nervous when you tell me, 'Get this done now.' I know it's old
feelings from my old job, and I'll get over it soon. I'd do better
with less pressure for now." Her boss expressed appreciation
for the feedback.

Terissa's comments were slight adaptations of Telling What
You Want. A new job situation such as Terissa's often makes
being assertive easier. You don't have a long history and pattern
of discouragement and failure. When you're in an old job, with
an old pattern, then delivering negative feedback is difficult. Because we hate to deliver the message, we don't. And because we

haven't done it, the pattern doesn't change. Finally we're forced to give negative feedback about behavior that has been going on for a year or more!

Telling someone they aren't doing well, particularly if you've been glossing over problems for a while, is difficult to initiate because you fear their response to you. Will they cry? Will they get angry and retaliate? Will they pout? Will they sue you? Will they hate you? Maybe they'll develop a bad attitude, complain to everyone else, and your whole team will turn against you. Some people have more trouble giving negative feedback to bosses, some to peers, and some to subordinates. In the assertive communication classes, participants will often say, "Yeah, but this is my boss. I can't say that to him." Sure you can. You can give negative and positive feedback to your boss just as you do to your subordinates. You might do it less frequently, but the need and the communication techniques are the same. One of the trendy new business buzzwords is *360-degree feedback*. The approach refers to the need for managers to get good, concise, clear, structured feedback from people all around them: at their side, above, and below them. You'll be on the leading edge if you ask for and deliver that kind of negative and positive feedback.

Sean and Gregor had been working together for a year. Gregor, a manager, had brought Sean into the organization from another state, as a supervisor. Sean was young, enthusiastic, and skilled. He really liked his job and worked hard. Gregor was very supportive, personally as well as professionally. Initially, the fit was good. But Gregor began to see some potential chinks as the honeymoon period waned. Because he felt responsible for Sean, who had moved thousands of miles for this job, Gregor was reluctant to start pointing out his concerns.

Months went by with very little negative feedback given by Gregor or received by Sean. Sean thought everything was going extremely well. Although the transition had been difficult for him, he was beginning to feel comfortable with his job and the move. He approached his six-month performance appraisal confidently because he had met weekly with his boss Gregor since his arrival and was given only positive information about his work.

From Gregor's perspective, there were definitely some ominous signs. He saw Sean as not having some of the necessary skills for the job, but covering the lack with overconfident bragging. Gregor saw many strengths, but was concerned about Sean's people skills. There had been many attitude and performance problems within Sean's department to start with, but now, six months later, they were still there.

The problem? Sean didn't have a clue that Gregor was seriously concerned about his performance; so concerned that he was thinking about moving Sean to a staff rather than a line position. Gregor, as a manager, had to suggest the change since he saw it as essential to improve the bottom line. But he knew Sean would be stunned, as well as hurt, angry, and disappointed. He also realized that Sean would no longer trust him. Belatedly, he realized that in his efforts to be supportive, to be a mentor as well as a boss, he had done Sean a disservice. If Gregor had given the negative feedback from the beginning, along with the positive, Sean might not be on the verge of losing his position. And Gregor wouldn't be in the very uncomfortable position of Telling It Like It Is all of a sudden.

What happened? Gregor's discomfort, regret, and desire to get it over with contributed to his starting the appraisal with a blast. He began by saying, "I should have told you before, but you're just not doing your job. You don't have the people skills you need to motivate your employees, so they're not doing their job. You just can't do what needs to be done, so I'm moving you into an individual contributor job instead of a supervisory job." He was definitely telling it like it is, but in a more aggressive rather than assertive manner. And way too late.

Sean was stunned, and the whole conversation and its consequences disjointed the entire organization for the next month. Sean lost trust in his boss. He wondered if this was the norm in the company. He worried that others thought little of him and hadn't told him as well. Other people who worked for Gregor lost faith in him as well. They worried that maybe he wasn't telling them some information about their performance.

It is so much easier for everyone and the organization to give people routine negative feedback. Give them positive feedback too. Both need to be specific, concise, and frequent. Positive feedback is underrepresented in most workplaces. A lack of pats on the back usually results from carelessness or forgetfulness rather than fear. A systematic approach to giving positive and negative feedback is requisite to cultivating superior performance.

The IMB MO for Telling It Like It Is

Deciding what you want is easy if an inability or unwillingness to give positive and/or negative feedback is the problem you're trying to solve. For the purpose of being clear about what you want, let's define feedback. The first dictionary definition comes from the vocabulary of the electrical field—the transfer of part of the output of an active circuit or device back to the input, either as an unwanted effect or in an intentional use, as to reduce distortion. Translating that definition into people-at-work talk instead of electrical lingo, feedback means to intentionally transfer back to someone information about their output, or behavior, in order to improve the accuracy of their perception about their performance. Receiving feedback is a useful process for the receiver.

The important part of Deciding What You Want, as it relates to Telling It Like It Is, is clarifying exactly who you want to do it with and in what situation. Is this only a problem for you with your boss, or is it a problem with everyone at work? Are you great at giving positive feedback when called for but hesitant to give negative feedback? Are you in that small group of people who always feels uncomfortable giving positive feedback? If you praise your boss, are you concerned she may see you as trying to win her over? If you praise your underlings, are you concerned they might see you as too easy going? Those concerns may be barriers to be dealt with later, but right now don't let them get in the way of Deciding What You Want. Remember the specific parts of that decision: the behavior, the specific person or persons, and the specific situation. Here are some sample goals for giving feedback:

- I want to be able to give negative feedback to my new hires the first time I notice a performance problem.
- I want to be able to give genuine positive feedback to all my coworkers at least once a week.
- I want to be able to give negative feedback to my boss in situations where his behavior toward me doesn't work well for me.
- I want to be able to tell a coworker that I don't like his dirty jokes, even though I've been listening to them and laughing at them for five years.

Determine your goal for this particular assertive communication area, and write it down clearly and measurably so you'll know you've accomplished it when it happens.

Identify the Negative Thinking

As individuals we all have our own idiosyncrasies. For example, some people would much rather be the receiver of negative feedback than have to give it; others are embarrassed to give positive feedback, thinking it presumptuous. But I've learned from my class participants that the type of negative thinking that goes on in Telling It Like It Is situations varies most depending on who you're wanting to tell and what you're wanting to tell them! People are most concerned about giving direct negative feedback to bosses because of their power and role and to nonassertive direct reports because of their perceived fragility.

The negative thinking that often takes place goes like this:

"I don't have the right to tell the boss anything but 'yes.' "
"He's the boss. I can't tell him what I really think."
"She won't take it well if I tell her she's just meeting expectations. It'll ruin her morale and then her performance will be even worse."
"He looks so sad all the time anyway. If I tell him something

negative about his performance he'll probably jump off a bridge!"

Giving positive feedback, hard as it may be to believe, is difficult for many people for a variety of reasons. If the praise goes to the boss, people may be concerned that it sounds phony or arrogant. If the positive comment is directed to a subordinate, the risk of sounding patronizing is a concern. Some of the internal monologues that can be a barrier to Telling It Like It Is in a positive way are:

"He doesn't care what I think."
"She'll just figure I'm trying to get in good with her."
"Who am I to tell my boss that she's doing well?"
"She doesn't need to hear from me that she's a quick learner. I'm sure she knows that already and it'll sound trite."
"I don't think he thinks I'm such a good supervisor anyway, so my opinion doesn't have any value to him."
"They'll just think I'm trying to push them to work harder by giving a big 'feel good' shot."

Substitute, Challenge, and Stop

To move yourself to take action and really deliver that feedback, positive or negative, in a systematic, frequent, and constructive way, you need to remove those internal thinking barriers as quickly and completely as possible. Although identifying each thought and stopping it, or substituting a more instructional thought, or challenging the thought, are all possible ways to overcome the barrier, reframing is probably the most efficient approach. If you're in a supervisory position and see an ongoing need to Tell It Like It Is, reframing the entire feedback process is the most effective way to terminally eliminate the negative thinking barrier.

The basis for most internal monologues about giving negative feedback to anyone about anything is that they won't receive it well. You project that they will think less of you in one way or another for Telling It Like It Is. You anticipate that their subsequent behavior will reflect their animosity toward you.

There are a variety of possible major reframes of the feedback situation.

- People generally appreciate getting clear, specific feedback, good or bad. They will respect you for delivering the clear message.
- You are doing people a favor by giving frequent, brief feedback, positive and negative. As you would probably rather know where you stand at all times, your subordinates would like to know.
- Not Telling It Like It Is is not an option. As a supervisor, giving direct feedback, often, is as much a part of your job expectation as doing performance appraisals on a yearly basis.
- Good communication in the work environment is valued highly by all employees. Being a good communicator is essential to success. Delivering clear feedback is essential to being a good communicator.
- In any job, there are functions that you enjoy and those you don't. By practicing, giving feedback can become a function that you enjoy.

If none of these new pictures works for you, then come up with your own. The point of reframing is that if you see the process differently, then you think about it differently and you behave and communicate differently, creating a new outcome.

If Gregor had reframed his thinking about Sean, from feeling responsible for him and therefore unable to criticize and possibly disappoint him to having a responsibility toward him and therefore giving him frequent, consistent negative and positive feedback, there would have been a much more pleasant outcome for both men and the organization.

Select a Technique

Telling What You Want

The best technique to use and adapt to the circumstances is Telling What You Want. Intrinsically, the technique is brief and specific. It also requires that you describe and not label the behavior or the situation that is of concern to you, so the listener's reaction is less defensive. Because you need to talk about your feelings as well as your thoughts, the technique also necessitates your thinking through your motivations and intentions. It also adds clarity for your target person. Finally, ending with what you want or what you'd like to see happen leaves the target person feeling more optimistic, positive, and forward looking.

Going back to the Gregor and Sean situation described at the beginning of the chapter, here are some Telling What You Want statements that Gregor could have made all along, rather than waiting for the performance appraisal to drop the bomb:

> "I'm concerned that you're spending a great deal of your time on administrative matters. I'd like you to be out in the field at least eight hours a week."
>
> "I'm uneasy about your ability to communicate directly and clearly with your people. I'd like you to take the effective listening skills class and then the assertive communication class that corporate offers."
>
> "I'm not satisfied with how things are going, Sean. I want you to do a better job changing attitudes and motivating people in the field. I'd be happy to help you do that, but it has to start happening."

Here are some other examples of giving negative feedback using Telling What You Want:

> "I'm concerned when you come to meetings late, twice in a row, and I'd like you to be on time for the staff meetings on a regular basis."
>
> "I'm getting angry about your not returning my calls within twenty-four hours or on the day you said you'd call. Follow-up and good communication is my top priority. I'd like you to keep a log of your communication with me for the next month so we can discuss the issue again."

If the situation is a recurring one and you've told the person once, or even twice, exactly what you want, and haven't received the results you expected, then it's time to add a consequence. The consequence needs to be just that—the anticipated outcome of continued success or lack of success on the part of your subordinate. This add-on shouldn't be used as an ultimatum or a threat. Don't even use it if you're not sure you can and will follow through if necessary. Here's what it should sound like, added on to one of the statements above, assuming you'd made the Telling What You Want statement before: "I've mentioned before that it concerns me when you answer my questions about the state of your team with 'Don't worry, everything's fine.' I've asked for more specific information and I still am not getting it. If this pattern continues, I want you to know that I'll put someone else in the position of team leader, someone who can give me that information in a timely and clear manner."

Similarly, you can use Telling What You Want for positive feedback. Here are some examples:

"I'm elated that you completed that budget projection so fast. I really want you to continue working on your number crunching because I see great progress and I think you have the knack."

"I'm comfortable with the way you handled the difficult situation with Mark. I appreciate your people skills and want them to be a continuing asset to our team."

Sometimes, people feel it's just too much work to go through the "I feel _____ when you _____ and I want _____" technique. Although Telling What You Want is preferred because it's descriptive and brief, using just a plain "I" statement also works.

"I think you handled that difficult situation extremely well."

"I'd like you to start coming to meetings on time, in a consistent manner."

"I want you to take some communication classes."

"I'd rather you spent more time out in the field and less time at the office."

Telling It Like It Is can be confused with brutal honesty. The most important aspect of delivering a message is delivering it in a way that it can be received. Brutal honesty generally isn't received well. People have to defend themselves against it. Consequently they don't hear it. Brutal honesty is saying, "Sean, your performance stinks." When I point out the harshness of a comment like that, people justify their behavior by saying, "But it's true." It may be true, but stating your opinion in that way accomplishes nothing productive. The person you're telling feels punished, but knows nothing that will help him or her move forward.

Saying "No"

The other technique that is important for people who need to work on Telling It Like It Is is saying "no," either as the initiator or as a responder. Until you learn to say "no" effectively, developing credibility as an "I Mean Business" communicator is almost impossible. In the situation between Gregor and Sean, how could Gregor have used saying "no" as an initiator early on in the relationship to avoid dumping it all at the performance appraisal? Some examples of what Gregor could have said early on, using a no-based "I" statement, are:

> "I'm not going to be micromanaging you and telling you exactly what to do and what not to do. It's not my style. I want you to take the initiative to check with me routinely about your ideas and actions."
> "I don't like my team leaders spending a lot of time hanging around the office. I want them out in the field gathering information, motivating people, being a role model, being a problem solver."

Remember

- Giving straightforward, direct, positive and negative feedback is a part of everyone's job description even if not written.
- Recognizing that most people appreciate getting clear

feedback will help you overcome the internal obstacles to
Telling It Like It Is.

- Telling What You Want or using plain "I" statements is
  the best way to deliver direct feedback.
- Telling It Like It Is delivers the message so that someone
  can receive it. Brutal honesty doesn't accomplish the same
  thing.

8
Intercepting the Indirect Hit

The Situation

Many people think the toughest communication situation to handle, and the one they'd most like to avoid, is conflict with an aggressive, competitive, hostile person. Even though the hard-nosed, sarcastic, intense, or put-down kind of person is definitely scary to deal with, often the indirectly aggressive communicator presents a more difficult, if less frightening, challenge.

There are a variety of situations where, if the words were written on paper, they wouldn't look critical, but when you hear them, they sound judgmental in an indirect way. Here's an example. You've gone out to lunch with a coworker who's also a good friend. You've had a fun time, talking business and personal stuff. You've been gone for almost an hour and a half. In your workplace, there is no clear rule about exactly how long you can take for lunch or what time you must come in or leave, but most people go out for lunch for an hour or else they eat lunch in. As you get off the elevator, having left your buddy a few floors below, a coworker says to you, "How did you enjoy your two-hour lunch?" On the surface and on the written page, that comment looks and sounds pretty innocent, but add the edgy tone of voice and the subtle body language—the *metacommunication* as it's called by linguists—and suddenly there's a real feel of criticism. Even if you're not supersensitive, the message may come across as if the person had said, "I noticed that you were gone for almost two hours and I strongly disapprove of that use of your time. I don't know who you were with or the purpose of your lunch, but I think what you were doing is not justifiable. I want to make you uncomfortable and make you feel guilty."

If the person had in fact said those words, deciding what to say in return would actually be simpler for you than responding to the "How did you enjoy your two-hour lunch?" question. You could say, "I appreciate your candor, but I think I'm the best judge of how I use my time," Or, "I feel uncomfortable about your telling me that you want me to feel guilty and I don't want to continue this conversation."

When someone talks to you so that the words sound OK but

the message seems to carry hostile undertones, you can easily be confused. The mixed message, a verbal message and a tone-of-voice message that doesn't fit the word message, can stop you in your tracks. You say or do nothing at the time, but you feel uncomfortable and criticized. Later, the message seems even less clear and you begin to doubt yourself. You wonder if maybe you're making a big deal out of nothing.

Another common mixed message is often delivered under the guise of concern for your well-being. A coworker, Yael, comes up to you and says, "Are you OK, Sonya?" You answer, "Yeah, I'm fine. What's the question about?" Yael answers, "Oh, I was just worried. You look exhausted and you seem so blah today. I thought maybe you were sick or something. Or maybe you had a family crisis. You just aren't yourself today." Meanwhile, you thought everything was pretty much fine. You feel OK and you aren't having any big problems, but now that Yael has mentioned your blahness, you begin to wonder if something is wrong that shows to others but you haven't noticed.

How do you deal with this kind of mixed message? On one hand, it sounds as if the person is caring and is expressing concern about your well-being. On the other hand, it seems to you that they're telling you that you look awful and are acting listless. It's hard to take that as a caring, nurturing message. What do you do? You're in a bind again.

A participant in a recent assertive communication class had a very subtle situation that seemed to involve indirect aggressiveness.

Tamaya works in a small printing company. The owners, her bosses, are a married couple, Sol and Marie. Tamaya's day generally begins at 7:00 A.M. She often opens the main office and deals with leftover paperwork and long distance phone calls before the rest of the staff arrives at about 9. She usually leaves at 5 or 5:30 in the afternoon.

On the other hand, the firm's owners arrive about 10 and often stay until 7 or 7:30 at night. On the particular day that Tamaya had the assertiveness class in the evening, she and the owners were following their usual pattern. Tamaya was getting ready to leave at 5, and as she walked by her boss Sol's office, he looked up, looked at his watch, tapped it and said, "Is your watch broken?"

Sol's question wasn't delivered in a hostile manner, nor in a humorous manner; rather in a matter-of-fact way. Tamaya didn't answer and kept on walking out of the building. But she didn't feel good. She didn't know what he was saying, or implying, or what his behavior meant. Was it a criticism of her leaving earlier than he thought she should leave or earlier than he leaves? Was Sol being sarcastic? Was he joking and just didn't come across that way? Did he truly not know that she generally was in at 7:00 A.M., so leaving at 5 P.M. was still a ten-hour day for her? Did he think employees, or Tamaya in particular, should work twelve-hour days?

Tamaya not only didn't know what Sol meant, but she also didn't know what she should say or do, so she said nothing. She thought of asking Sol what he meant. She wondered about just saying, "I was here at 7 this morning." She considered telling Sol that his comment had upset her. She also thought about asking him why he had asked her that question, but she remembered that asking "why" always puts people on the defensive and she didn't want Sol to feel criticized. Tamaya wasn't comfortable with any of the options she considered, so she left and came to class, where she asked us for advice.

The IMB MO for Dealing With Indirect Hits

Responding to the indirect hit is difficult for many people. It often throws you off guard and you can't react very quickly. You're so busy analyzing it that by the time you think you've figured out what happened, it's too late to say anything. The situation has passed. Even if you finally decide what to say, bringing it up an hour or a day later can seem like shooting a fly with a cannon.

Decide What You Want

In the indirect hit situation, once you understand exactly what's going on and why you feel so on edge after one of these mixed messages, you may decide that the best way to handle it is to just let it go. If you are bothered by the comments, and someone at work delivers the indirect assault frequently, with skill and apparent relish, then maybe you want them to stop doing it. Usually deciding what we want for ourselves works much better than deciding what we want from other people, because we have control over us and not over them. But if you do want them to stop, then you may want to think of something that you can say or do to increase the likelihood that they will stop.

Identify the Negative Thinking

Often the negative thinking that results from the indirect hit is different from most other internal monologues. If you don't notice anything strange about the other person's communication, then you treat the comment matter-of-factly and just respond. But if and when you notice what seems to be a zing and a sting, then a flood of internal thoughts are released. "Is that comment meant to be nasty? Is it well intentioned and I'm being paranoid? Should I take it personally? Or would that be an overreaction? Should I be offended? Or insulted? Or am I sounding defensive, even to myself? Should I just ignore the comment and hope it goes away? What should I say if I decide to say anything?"

The internal questioning usually stops people from acting because they're trying to figure out what's going on. The first time someone new zings you, responding on the spot is almost impossible. You're analyzing and translating. First you have to recognize that a mixed message has in fact been delivered. Then you have to figure out how to respond. Once you've successfully intercepted the hit and interrupted the pattern, your own internal monologue, which can paralyze you, eventually disappears. Once you've successfully dealt with the indirect hit, the assaulter is much less likely to give you a second mixed message, that day or subsequently.

Substitute, Challenge, and Stop

When you know that someone has a habit of delivering the indirect assault, then you don't have to waste a second analyzing or interpreting. You recognize the mixed message in a shot and you know what to do. Your internal dialogue is much less likely to get in the way. You don't hesitate and question the motives. You don't wonder whether you should take it personally. You just quickly substitute and give yourself good instructions. "OK. I recognize that as a mixed message. I can respond with a straightforward answer, as if the message is a straightforward message. Or I can use an 'I feel _____ when you _____ and I want _____' comment, followed by Broken Record if necessary. That's it!"

But, when a new indirect assaulter appears, you'll probably be confused again, and go through the same negative thinking once again. Trust your gut. When you feel your own natural emotional response, stop the internal monologue, the analysis and questioning about the person's intentions or your possible overreaction, and move quickly into substitute mode. "I'll let this pass today. Next time I'll pick it up faster and give myself good, quick instructions about what to say."

Select a Technique

Eliminate the "Why" Question

Once you recognize the mixed message of the comment or question delivered by the indirectly aggressive communicator, the natural question is, "Why would she say that?" The next step might be to ask, "Why did you ask me if my watch was broken?" or "Why did you ask me if I enjoyed my two-hour lunch?" You genuinely may want to ascertain his or her motivation to determine whether you are being supersensitive or they are being supercritical in an indirect way.

Eliminating the "why" is even more fitting in response to the indirectly aggressive communicator because in its own way, "why" is perceived and received as a criticism. So you end up responding to an implied criticism with an implied criticism. And the answer to the "why" question probably doesn't get you where you want to go; not if you want to stop the mixed messages.

The "I" Statement

There are two main ways to deal with the indirect assault. The first technique is to use an "I" statement, or a slight variation, to answer the question asked. You act as if the message were straightforward rather than mixed and you answer accordingly. In answer to the question from Yael that seemed like a mixed message, "Are you OK, Sonya?", you would answer, "I'm fine." Or you could say, "I'm OK," or "I'm feeling great." That's the end of the conversation about the topic of you and how you're doing. You would then continue doing what you were doing or going where you were going. You could wait to see if Yael had anything else he wanted to talk to you about. Or you might bring up a different subject if some business needed to be discussed.

Similarly, in answer to the "Is your watch broken?" question mentioned earlier, you would simply say, "I think it's working well," and keep on going toward the door. The "How did you enjoy your two-hour lunch?" question can be answered simply. "I enjoyed it," or "It was great," or even, "I enjoyed the food, but the restaurant was noisy." You're just answering the question literally, ignoring the subtle other message, which may or may not be intended as criticism.

The advantage of this simple "I" response is that you can avoid getting into an unnecessary hassle. If there is a hidden message, you don't give the person the satisfaction of knowing that his indirectly aggressive communication produced good results, for him. You don't want him to learn that he was successful in rattling your cage with his mixed message. You don't want to give him the opportunity to retreat, look innocent, and leave you feeling as if you've overreacted. If there is a legitimate concern about your long lunch, your health, or your leaving work on time, the person will be forced to deal with the issue more directly. If there is no legitimate concern, then you've avoided being manipulated.

Telling What You Want and Broken Record

If the indirect assault seems to be a consistent pattern of communication with a coworker, or you've tried the brief "I" statement response to no avail, then I'd move on to Telling What You Want. In response to the lunch question you might say, "I feel uncomfortable when you ask me about my two-hour lunch. I'd like you to let me know directly if my going out for a long lunch is a problem from your point of view."

Inevitably, the indirect hitter denies bad intent. "Of course I don't have a problem with how long you take for lunch. It's none of my business. What are you so paranoid about?" Then you jump in with Broken Record rather than answering the question about paranoia. "I just want you to know how I felt when you said that to me about the two-hour lunch." If the communicator continues with his denial of bad motives and accusations of oversensitivity, you continue with Broken Record. "Perhaps you didn't mean it negatively, but I did feel criticized." Similarly with the broken watch comment, you would say, "I'm concerned when you ask if my watch is broken. If you are unhappy about my leaving at 5:30 today, or in general, I'd like you to tell me."

Another kind of denial response that you might get from the indirect assaulter is, "Don't be so sensitive. I'm just kidding. Can't you take a joke?" Again, use the Broken Record technique, rather than answering the question. "I would appreciate your telling me in the future if there is a problem about when I come in or leave."

Then, as before with the "I" statement, you get on with whatever you were doing. You say what you have to say, not to initiate a discussion, but to give the other person some information. You don't want to get into right or wrong, good or bad, intentions or motivations. You just want to attempt to stop an established pattern or prevent a pattern from developing.

Fogging and Negative Inquiry

Although the two communication techniques just covered are the most effective to eliminate future indirect hits, you might use a slight Fog or Negative Inquiry with some of the questions raised. Responding to the lunch question, you could Fog the person and say, "It was a long lunch." Or when Tamaya was asked about her watch being broken, she could have used negative inquiry and responded, "Is there something about my leaving now that is of concern?"

You'll find which technique or combination of techniques works best for you. Then you'll use that particular one until you get tired of it or it no longer works for you, or you decide you want to broaden your repertoire.

Remember

- Letting go of the indirect hit comment in communicating is OK if you can let it go in your head.
- If you feel criticized and confused by an apparent mixed message, trust your intuition.
- Don't ask the "why" question.
- Answering the mixed message question literally with an "I" statement is the simplest approach.
- Telling What You Want, followed by Broken Record, works well for interrupting a pattern, but may be more involvement than you want.
- Fogging and Negative Inquiry can also be quick ways out of the indirect hit situation.

9
Take Me Seriously

The Situation

"I want to be taken seriously at work," is a common clamor of new employees, young employees, and female employees who work in a male-dominated environment. "Taking someone or something seriously" is a frequently used phrase in the U.S. business culture. But exactly what it means to be taken seriously or to take someone seriously is not easily identified. The dictionary doesn't use the term "take seriously," but under "serious" several definitions add meaning: having earnestness or deep thought, meaning what one says or does, sincere, not joking or trifling. Taking those words, which define the adjective *serious*, and stretching to define the adverb *seriously*, taking someone seriously may mean treating them earnestly, sincerely, and as someone who is respected. Still, there are two components to being taken seriously: the employee behaving in a way that people perceive as deserving of attention and respect and the co-workers or employer behaving in a way that the employee perceives as respectful. How must new, young, and/or female workers behave in order to be taken seriously? And how can people indicate that they take those coworkers or direct reports seriously? The answer to the first question is one you have control over; the answer to the second question is less in your control.

A twenty-eight-year-old woman, Makeesha, has just been promoted to acting manager of an important, complex, and central department of a large, traditionally male-oriented organization. She has been promoted from a supervisory position that she held successfully for eight years. As a supervisor, her job was less supervisory than technical, so she comes to the job with little in the way of management skills but a good understanding of the intricacies of the department, its functions and technical demands.

No one else who applied for the job was better qualified technically or had the same length of experience as Makeesha. Other outside applicants had more management experience, but the company basically wanted to stay within its own ranks.

The VP who hired Makeesha had some concerns about her skill level, but he wanted to provide an opportunity for her development because he thought she had potential. He also saw the need to begin to bring more women into management in his predominantly male organization. The other management-level people were either much more experienced, much older, or much more highly educated than Makeesha. Everyone accepted her promotion into the acting position, genuinely wished success for her, wanted to be supportive, but had strong reservations about whether she could do the work. There was a strong wait-and-see attitude.

Makeesha had mixed feelings. She was delighted to have the opportunity to take on the manager position, but was not happy with the wait-and-see attitude of her peers and the clear reservations of her boss. She felt she was not being taken seriously. When Makeesha talked about her dissatisfaction with her title, she sounded complaining and whiny to her coworkers. When she talked about her strong skills and experience in the technical realm, she came across as not understanding the magnitude of the management challenge in front of her. When she attempted to sound positive and confident, she sounded immature and naive to the experienced managers. Makeesha's lack of knowledge of internal politics and the big corporate picture, which she demonstrated occasionally in large group meetings, contributed to her coming across as someone who "just doesn't get it"; someone that other managers don't take seriously.

The male managers, young and old, had trouble dealing with Makeesha. Although their intentions were good, their concern about hurting her feelings, or offending her, or damaging her self-esteem often got in the way of their giving her the straightforward feedback she needed.

When Makeesha gave a presentation that was overly detailed in tasks accomplished and noticeably light on action plans, no one told her what she needed to do differently next time. Her male coworkers helped her with the computer graphics and the overhead projection but weren't direct with her about her communication skills. Because they overprotected her in this way and shielded her from the blasting badinage they used with each other, they appeared to not be taking her seriously.

When Makeesha spoke up in a group meeting, her peers were generally polite, but few people argued, presented opposing viewpoints, or took her on directly. Without meaning to be, the men were somewhat patronizing. Later, among themselves, they talked about how much change and growth she needed to accomplish in a short period of time. When Makeesha didn't speak up in meetings, she was usually ignored.

In general, Makeesha didn't feel taken seriously, although she recognized that she did have some support from her peers. Her colleagues, although they wished her success and were willing to help if and when she took the initiative and proved her motivation and determination, probably didn't take her as seriously as they took each other. She didn't have the history, the power, the political savvy, or experience that many of the men had. And they weren't sure she would or could get the big picture.

Clearly, this is a complex problem that a couple of assertive communication techniques, injected at the right time and place, aren't going to solve quickly. Nonetheless the burden is on the employee who doesn't perceive he or she is being taken seriously to communicate in a way that increases the likelihood of the serious response taking place.

The IMB MO for Being Taken Seriously

A bit more finesse is required in Deciding What You Want when your concern is being taken seriously. You really need to give some thought to what being taken seriously would look and sound like if it happened. Even if you should decide to tell your coworkers or boss exactly what you want—to be taken more seriously—they and you might have an entirely different view of what taking someone seriously means. You need to know exactly what you want as responses toward you. Knowing what you want from others helps clear up your thinking and separate realistic from unrealistic expectations.

Perhaps being listened to, with head nods and verbal acknowledgment of your comments, is enough to make you feel taken seriously. Maybe you need praise and approval to feel taken seriously. Possibly you need to get the same treatment from your male coworkers that the rest of the men get. Maybe you would like people to give you open, direct, honest feedback, negative and positive, on a frequent basis. Perhaps you want all that and more.

When you want to be taken seriously, you also need to decide how to behave to increase the likelihood of getting the response you want. Are you willing to be that kind of person? Do you want to stop being a loose cannon if that's what it takes? Do you want to communicate more concisely? Do you want to learn to be more thick-skinned? Describe what you want from yourself as well as what you want from others in as clear and measurable terms as possible. As with other wants and goals, the more specific you can be, the greater are the chances that you can know you've achieved what you want.

Identify the Negative Thinking

When you don't feel taken seriously in the workplace, a lot of the internal thinking can revert to the same kind of childlike and even childish thought patterns that we had when we felt devalued as kids. We can feel foolish and ashamed, and we can also feel defensive and resentful. Some common internal thoughts of the new, less experienced worker are:

"They treat me like a kid."
"I must be some kind of joke to them."
"I'm so insignificant to them I feel like a nonperson."
"They must think I don't know anything."
"I'm never going to be accepted by this gang."
"They don't give me credit for what I've done."
"They act as if I don't even exist."

Usually people who feel not taken seriously in the workplace are the "I'm not good enough" kind of negative thinker. But the initiation of a new, young, inexperienced, or minority person into a majority-dominant workplace can unglue even the "they're not good enough" thinker. They tend to get more resentful and defensive whereas the more nonassertive thinking person tends to be more ashamed and embarrassed and insecure. Some internal thinking patterns that may go on with the more aggressive communicator are:

> "They think they're real hot shots. They don't know it all either."
>
> "Who do they think they are to act so superior?"
>
> "They had to start somewhere too, but they've obviously forgotten that."

The negative thinking results in behavior that doesn't improve the situation. The embarrassed, ashamed people tend to shut down and become more and more invisible to avoid further treatment as insignificant. The more aggressive people attempt to fight back by arguing, taking unpopular positions perhaps for the sake of being visible, being quick on the defensive trigger, and occasionally attacking the group or individuals in it. Neither approach works, and the negative thinking continues. So does the not-being-taken-seriously response.

Substitute, Challenge, and Stop

A few assertive communication techniques alone aren't going to accomplish your goal of being taken seriously. Similarly, a few substitute or reframed thoughts aren't going to solve this negative thinking problem either. This situation calls for a reduction in the negative thinking, of course, but also more of a problem-solving approach to coming up with a plan.

The altered thinking that you want to end up with will be neutral and instructional. When you find yourself in the situation where you don't feel taken seriously, rather than reverting to the old pattern, you say to yourself:

> "I'm handling this well."
>
> "I see what's happening and I'm dealing with it."
>
> "Keep my mind, right now, on the task at hand."

"One step at a time; I can handle the situation."

"I'm not getting pushed around, but I'm not going haywire either."

"They're telling me something about them and the culture, as well as something about me."

Reframing the not-being-taken-seriously situation is also a possibility, particularly if you're new, quite young relatively speaking, or someone who isn't out of the same mold as the majority members of the group. Instead of viewing what goes on as your not being taken seriously, you can view it as being hazed or initiated, both processes that have a clear beginning and a clear ending.

By reframing the situation as a normal part of joining a group that's already formed, you can take the not being listened to, the being put down or ignored, less personally. You can diminish the magnitude of what goes on by recognizing that slowly, over time, you'll probably pass the test, you'll be a full-fledged member of the group and be taken seriously. There's always the possibility that you won't pass muster, ever, but that outcome is unlikely. "I'll concentrate on the probabilities, not the possibilities," is a good substitute statement to make when you find yourself looking too closely at too many unlikely possibilities.

Because this situation is ongoing rather than an event, a conversation, or a comment, you'll need to really think through it and come up with a long-range solution that you feel confident is best for you. The solution may have a variety of components, only one of which may be improving your communication so that you are more open and direct. You may decide that to be taken more seriously you need to get more education or training, you need to develop mentors or sponsors, or you need to be more visible in the corporation and less visible in your department for the moment. You may conclude that you should become more politically sophisticated, better aligned within and outside of your department. You may decide that the best thing for you to do is put your nose to the grindstone and be the best new manager the organization has. Your boss and peers will have to take you more seriously when your production is up, your quality is up, and your errors are down.

To sift through the approaches and strategies, you may need to find someone outside of your department who's familiar with the corporate culture to help you problem solve. When that process has been accomplished successfully, you'll find it relatively easy to substitute for your old negative thinking pattern and move on to picking some communication techniques that you can use to feel serious, act serious, and increase the taking-you-seriously responses from your coworkers.

Select A Technique

Brief and Specific

Although being Brief and Specific is an important component of all other assertive communication techniques, using specific words to fit specific situations contributes to being taken seriously. For example, to say, "I told him he needed to get his act together," isn't as powerful as saying, "I told him he needed to bring his sales production up by March first." If someone asks what your opinion is about a good meeting time, saying, "Whatever," is less serious sounding than saying, "Monday is better for me." If it really doesn't make a difference to you, saying, "Either day is fine," is better than, "Whatever," or "It doesn't matter," or "A-a-a-nh."

Using precise words, not trite words, and occasionally unusual words may enhance others' perception of you. There are many overused words and phrases in the business culture. The words *challenge* and *opportunity* are often used as fake synonyms for a great big, huge problem! The buzz words *reengineering, culture, team,* and *empowerment* can have entirely different meanings to different people and groups. Work at being a concise and clear communicator, not a clone of the spin doctors in the organization. Using a word that is new to the group, not necessarily a ten-syllable word, can aid in people seeing you as intelligent and capable. A good vocabulary is often perceived, correctly or not, as a sign of smarts. Using the words *predicament, dilemma,* or *impasse* instead of *problem* might begin to alter others' response.

Eliminate Disclaimers and Apologies

In the situation described early in the chapter, Makeesha was the new and inexperienced manager. In order to thwart what she perceived, accurately, as coworkers' perception that she didn't know what she was doing, Makeesha began every sentence with a disclaimer or apology.

"Perhaps I should have figured this out myself, but. . . ."
"I'm sorry that we don't have the up-to-date data that you need, but. . . ."
"I guess I should have been more aware of all the errors, but. . . ."

Beginning a sentence with a disclaimer is an attempt to keep other people from making a critical comment to you. Makeesha hopes, not consciously, that if she makes the criticism or apology at the beginning, her boss won't make it at the end. Unfortunately, what the listener usually hears is Makeesha validating what he already thinks—that she's not very good at her job.

By eliminating all the excess, preliminary wording, you can get to the point more quickly. You can also sound more certain and confident, which increases the likelihood that other people will see you as competent and take you seriously.

Reduce Details

Decreasing the details and potential rambling in a conversation is another useful technique for people who want to be taken seriously. Talking in brief, short sentences that end in periods comes across as serious. Linking several thoughts with "and" sounds disorganized. Here's the difference: "I've decided to attend a performance management workshop to improve my management skills" is the concise version. "I'm thinking that maybe I should go to a workshop to help me with my management skills and there's one being put on by the community college on performance management that sounds pretty good and I'd like to see if it would help with some of the challenges I'm having to handle now" is the excessively detailed and rambling

approach. The first statement definitely sounds more convincing. The person comes across as a person to be reckoned with, a
serious person who knows what she wants.

"I" Statements

For someone who wants to be taken seriously, telling other
people clearly and straightforwardly what you think, or believe,
or feel is necessary. Although in many situations asking questions is essential for the new or young person in the division,
don't do it in the staff meeting or the group problem-solving
session unless the question is purely data collection. Here's the
difference: "Do you all think that we can really alter this situation?" sounds somewhat uncertain and helpless. It attempts to
develop agreement on a topic when the speaker doesn't have
much power. "Joe, do you have the report on response time with
you?" is purely gathering information and doesn't sound helpless or like an attempt to sound overly confident.

Sometimes newcomers to the workplace react to not being
taken seriously by proclaiming their capabilities. "I've had a lot
of experience before with this kind of problem. I was practically
raised on personnel problems. Both my parents and my older
brother are HR people, so I know the ropes."

Although this "I" statement is fairly brief and is an opinion,
it's best not said because it appears immature at best and cocky
at worst. It would be better to just state your opinion about the
solutions to the problem. "I think we have to set firmer limits
about sick time. If someone goes home sick any time during his
shift, that counts as a sick day."

Undoubtedly, someone with a longer history with the company will say something like, "We tried that and it didn't work,"
or the latest quick quip, "Been there, done that." You'll probably
feel not taken seriously with that comment, but the best thing to
do is to kick in your healthy thinking, "I can handle this. One
step at a time." Then, you can decide if you want to just let the
idea go for now, use Broken Record to say it in a slightly different way, or use Fogging to defuse the rebuff in a positive way.
"I probably could come up with a more original solution."

Telling What You Want

Telling What You Want is a somewhat risky technique to use when you want to be taken seriously because you open yourself up more by expressing your feelings. But because the technique does require some bravery in this situation, you may enhance your coworkers' respect for you.

A funny (in retrospect, not at the time) circumstance happened when I attempted to be taken seriously by a group of male attorneys. They had invited me to meet with them about gender issues in their large law firm. As I entered the meeting room, no one looked around or introduced themselves. I sat down at the large conference table. I wasn't offered the coffee or fruit that the men were all ingesting.

During the meeting, someone would request my opinion about an issue, then tell me that I was wrong. They argued every point with me, disputed my sources, cut up the research I cited. They would ask me a question, and then answer it among themselves. The conversation was fast-paced, loud, and to me, somewhat hostile.

I was uncomfortable and felt like I was playing a losing game. I didn't think that I was being taken very seriously. I was becoming anxious and wanted to interrupt the pattern. I decided to take a risk and use Telling What I Want. So I said, "I'm beginning to feel anxious. I came here at your invitation to help you solve or prevent some problems, but I'm being treated like an adversary. I'd like you to recall the reason you asked me to come in and consult with you so we can better reach the outcome that you want."

The response was a lot of laughter and a comment, "That's what we're paying you for, to get stressed out." My retort was the only one of the morning that shut them up: "I'm not being paid." However, shortly after my comment and retort, the head honcho attorney, with an overly apologetic disclaimer about an important meeting with a judge that he had to attend, left the room and the meeting ended.

Would I use that technique again? Probably so. As in many uncomfortable discussions, when I take action, I feel better even if I don't get what I say I want. I felt better, leaving the room, having made a content-to-process switch (where one switches the focus from the attacking content to the communication process between that person and the aggressive communicator, discussed in more detail in Chapter 10), and having made some small impact, than if I had just continued to allow the not-being-taken-seriously conversation to continue.

How might you use Telling What You Want? If every time you put an idea out, the response is a bored yawn, a sigh, and "Been there, done that," you might say, "I'm frustrated when you tell me that you've been there and done that when I present what to me is a new idea. I'd appreciate your giving me some information about what or why or how it didn't work so I can learn from your experience." That's a slight adaptation of "I feel _____ when you _____ and I want _____." You use the feeling word (*frustrated*) straight out and you use *appreciate* instead of *want*, but the basic structure works.

If no one ever seems to acknowledge your comments, positively or negatively, you could say, "I feel isolated when no one in the meeting responds in any way to comments I make. I'd like something back even if it's a grunt. I'd even rather have criticism than nothing." A little humor can help in this and all tough situations.

Remember

Not being taken seriously is a major concern of a broad spectrum of employees. Try to find someone who's in the same dilemma, and pool resources, techniques, and solutions. You'll maintain a healthier perspective.

- This circumstance is of a longer duration than the one-time comment, or the one-person communication problem, so dealing with it takes more time, more energy, and more resilience.
- Identifying exactly what you want to happen, as the initiator of being taken seriously behavior or in response to indicate that you are being taken seriously, is essential.

That way you'll know you're always working toward achieving the desired outcome. Identifying the response you want as an indication of being taken seriously will keep you from generalizing all responses as further indication of the problem.

- Being brief, concise, and specific and eliminating excessive words, details, disclaimers, and apologies is the single most important communication combination.
- Keep the faith. Everyone goes through this kind of situation more than once in their lifetime. Most live to laugh about it in retrospect.

10
Surviving the Aggressive Attack

The Situation

Working with a hostile, aggressive, loud communicator is one of the toughest challenges for even a good, confident, direct communicator. The good news is that the situation is not cloaked in secrecy or uncertainty. You don't have to be afraid of the unknown. You don't need to worry that a confrontation might take place. You know what's going to happen—frequent, frightening, belligerent blowups. You also know that no matter what you do or say and no matter how well you handle the situation, the hostile, loud stuff will probably continue, unless you acquire more position power than the yeller.

Here is the usual, if somewhat exaggerated example. The aggressive communicator is a man, a boss type, often in middle or upper management. He thinks he is right most, if not all, of the time. He thinks that being right gives him the right to say what he wants to say in whatever manner he wants to say it. He thinks that his position entitles him to be dictatorial and arbitrary. As a matter of fact, he may think that he's doing all his direct reports a favor by being honest with them, by not mincing words, by letting them know at all times where they stand. He may truly believe that his management style is best and may see less autocratic or forceful managers as wimps. He has minimal awareness of the impact of his behavior on the people he views as his subordinates.

> A group of supervisors was given incorrect information about upcoming benefit changes by two managers, Neil and Glynda. After the error was discovered, the big boss, Sam, delivered the correct information to the supervisors at a scheduled meeting and during the meeting summoned the managers to his office.
>
> Although no names were mentioned or criticisms leveled directly at Glynda and Neil during the meeting with supervisors, the looks and obvious omissions by Sam conveyed the message loud and clear that there had been a major screwup. The supervisors also knew without a doubt exactly who Sam held responsible and who was going to pay the price—their bosses, Glynda and Neil.

Sam and the two managers walked silently to his office. Sam sat on one side of his desk, the managers on the other side facing him. Sam began, leaning forward across his desk, looking fairly fierce. "Well?" Neil and Glynda both started talking at once, nervously attempting to explain what had happened. Booming across the desk and interrupting them, Sam said, "Don't give me that whining, sniveling crap. There's no explanation that you can possibly give me that would make sense or make the situation OK. You screwed up big time and there's no excuse.

Both managers sat quietly in their chairs. The room was silent. Again Sam shouted, "Why didn't either of you figure out that you had wrong information. Any idiot could have used common sense and determined that the numbers you were giving out were totally out of whack. And to have both of you stumbling along without a clue. Talk about the blind leading the blind!"

Again silence. Sam continued in an intense manner, "Don't either of you have anything to say? What's the problem? Why are you sitting there like bumps on a log?" Neil answered quietly and tentatively, "I don't really know what to say. I can't really explain what happened. I have a cold and I'm really not feeling very well and I wasn't feeling well when we went over the information yesterday and. . . ."

Sam interrupted, "Why should I care if you're sick? That has nothing to do with the situation. I care that you two both distributed wrong information. And you damn well better figure out something to say because from my point of view this whole event is inexcusable. Here we are trying to build some trust in the organization, and you tell your people lies. I don't know how you're going to get out of this one, but you better figure it out."

Again silence. Sam got up and said, "I'm leaving. You two are hopeless." The three of them left the office together. Sam left the building, and Neil and Glynda went to their respective offices.

Is this good communication? Is this unusual communication? Unfortunately, in many companies, large and small, there are pockets where this type of aggressive communication is sanctioned, if not admired. It's not considered good, but it's also not considered unusual.

The IMB MO for Dealing With Aggressive Assaults

Generally anyone who is the object of aggressive assault knows exactly what he or she wants: to get out now! In personal situations and even in some work situations, we can do just that. We can get up and walk out the door, even get in our car and leave until the person calms down and cools off. But in the workplace, when the hostile, put-down person is the boss, people generally can't walk away without dire consequences. Maybe what you want is truly just to survive the assault in the practical sense and not get fired, transferred, or demoted. Maybe what you want is to survive in the psychological sense. You want to emerge without feeling like you've been run over by a truck. You want to emerge with your self-esteem at least hovering above zero.

If you're beginning to think that what you really want is to win in this kind of situation, then you need to think again. You really can't win without losing. With most aggressive communicators, there is no such thing as a win-win. If they don't beat you, they think they've lost. And then they're even more resentful.

My recommendation for dealing with the aggressive boss is that your goal be simply survival. Stating the goal clearly and in the form that was suggested in Chapter 2, you might say: I want to be able to leave this discussion with my boss, where he puts me down and is intense and critical, and feel calmer and more comfortable and confident about myself than I do now.

Identifying the Negative Thinking

The negative thinking that gets in the way of coping with someone who seems to be attacking you personally is fairly simple and similar for "I'm not good enough" thinkers as well as "Why bother" thinkers. Most people are frightened by loud, hostile critical communication. They are also scared by confrontation.

Their thinking is consequently often irrational and fragmented, focused on their emotional reaction and reflecting their high state of anxiety: "My heart is racing. I can't even think." "He really looks ticked off. Even more than ever. Oh God. I can't handle this." "I'm paralyzed. I can't even talk." "I know I'm going to cry. I can't cope with this. I'm going to fall apart." Other aggressive communicators may also be somewhat intimidated by the challenging, hostile manner represented by Sam, but they usually aren't as fearful as nonassertive communicators because they're more familiar with and therefore comfortable with the adrenaline flow, the intensity, and the loudness. Aggressive communicators are attacked less frequently and less directly by other aggressive communicators than are nonassertive communicators. Consequently, their negative thinking may be totally different from that of the "I'm not good enough" or the "Why bother?" people. Their natural internal monologue style of "You're not good enough" works well for them in this particular situation: "There goes Sam being an asshole again." "Who does he think he is, acting so superior?" "What a jerk." "He's spouting off again."

Thinking in that way helps the aggressive listener stay somewhat detached from the aggressive communicator, not take the aggressive communication too personally, and not get into combative mode. The normal blaming-others thinking in this case isn't negative thinking for the aggressive listener. It actually aids in doing what he or she needs to do to survive—stay calm and not compete.

Substitute, Challenge, and Stop

When your body is reacting physiologically to intense and hostile communication, your brain almost automatically starts giving you a printout about what's going on: "Whoa. The heart's racing. You're getting short of breath. You've got a knot in your stomach." In most situations of actual physical danger, that automatic readout is useful. You can use it to keep close track of your body and determine what you should or shouldn't, can or can't accomplish physically to cope with the danger.

In a high-stress communication confrontation, the flashing

lights in your brain aren't as helpful. They get in the way of your doing what you need to do, which is to stay calm, cool, and in control. Remembering that eliminating the negative thinking is more important than substituting positive thinking, the assault situation is a perfect time to call on your Stop skills. Imagine that Stop sign in your head. All those negative thoughts come to a screeching halt confronted by the red and white hexagonal Stop sign. Or turn the volume down, erase them, pack them up in a garbage bag for the moment. But get them out of the way so you can begin to chill out.

In the high-intensity assault situation, the best reaction on your part is to stay focused and listen. In order to accomplish that task well, you need to slow down physiologically and emotionally. The most effective form of cognitive restructuring to use is one short coping statement that you say repetitively to yourself during the entire attack:

"I can stay calm, cool, and in control."
"Relax. I'll be OK."
"I'm hanging in, being calm."
"Just breathe evenly and slowly."

Another coping statement that helps you to acquire some distance and detachment from the intensity of a confrontation is to say to yourself, "He's telling me something about him, not about me." Or "There's Sam just being Sam." In a way, you're adopting, for this kind of situation, an adaptation of the normal negative thinking of an aggressive communicator. But for you, similarly to the aggressive listener in a confrontation with an aggressive communicator, the thinking isn't negative. It doesn't get in your way of doing what you want to do. It actually helps you to stay calm. Mentally placing the responsibility on the other person helps you to remove yourself emotionally for the moment and avoid the self-defeating thinking or behaving that results from overemotional and overphysiological involvement with an aggressor.

Select a Technique

Given that what you want in the assault situation is to survive with some self-esteem intact, then only a limited number of techniques are useful. Often the aggressive communicator is handled most effectively by using indirect influence techniques, not the direct influence techniques of assertiveness. But that's another book.

Eliminate Disclaimers and Apologies

When someone is angry, frustrated, and critical of you and they're communicating their thoughts to you in an aggressive manner, saying you're sorry doesn't help. Giving a lot of detailed disclaimers and qualifiers also doesn't usually decrease the assault. "I'm really sorry. I don't know how that happened. We usually have all the correct information and have gone over it with each other carefully before we make a presentation. It really isn't our pattern to have that kind of misinformation get past us. I promise, it'll never happen again." Although you may be conveying absolutely correct information, the details and apologies often add fuel to a fire rather than cool it off.

Fogging

Admitting that there might be some truth to what the attacker is saying to you is a good way to buy some time and to begin to de-escalate the intensity of a hostile situation. You don't fold, admit defeat, or take all the blame. You just acknowledge that you could have behaved or thought differently. If your boss accuses you of being too detail-oriented, you could Fog her by saying, "I do occasionally overlook the big picture." If a coworker tells you that you seemed nervous during your presentation, you can use Fogging by saying, "I am fairly tense when I present." The purpose of Fogging is to buy you some time, perhaps stop the direction of the conversation, and decrease the potential for escalation of intensity. Fogging also prevents you from getting defensive, trying to justify your behavior, and provoking an increasingly harsh attack.

Looking back to the situation described with Sam, his first clear criticism went thus: "Don't give me that whining, sniveling crap. There's no explanation that you can possibly give me that would make sense or make the situation OK. You screwed up

big time and there's no excuse." There are a variety of ways
you could Fog: "We do sound somewhat helpless." "I probably
could have a better explanation than what I gave you."

The best Fog is to just deal straight on with the goof and
say, "We could have done a better job of getting and validating
the data before we presented it to the supervisors." The comment doesn't make everything smooth, but it interrupts the
usual back-and-forth pattern: He attacks; you defend; he height-
ens the attack; you increase the defense.

The other frequent pattern is attack, no response, attack, no
response, attack, defeat. By Fogging, you at least respond, which
helps you to feel that you're maintaining some control and dig-
nity in the situation. When you use a combination of Fogging,
Negative Inquiry, Broken Record, and Telling What You Want,
you generally feel OK at the end of the conversation. When you
use only apologetic, defensive, and justifying responses, you
usually feel exhausted, hopeless, and defeated at the end of the
conversation.

Negative Inquiry

In the aggressive assault situation, Negative Inquiry can
serve a similar purpose to Fogging. It interrupts the pattern of
defensiveness and further attack, and increases the likelihood
that you as the attackee will leave the situation with more information as well as more self-esteem.

Going back to a different point in the Sam conversation,
Sam shouts, "Well, why didn't either of you figure out that you
had wrong information. Any idiot could have used common
sense and determined that the numbers you were giving out
were totally out of whack. And to have both of you stumbling
along without a clue. Talk about the blind leading the blind!"
This comment could be Fogged. Neil could say, "We could have
thought through the information more carefully." Or, using
Negative Inquiry here, Glynda might say, "What most concerns
you about our giving the wrong information to the supervisors?" The additional advantage of the Negative Inquiry here is
that is refocuses the direction of the conversation from Neil and
Glynda to the consequences of their behavior on the supervisors.

It also moves Sam more toward looking realistically at how bad the consequences are rather than at how ticked off he is at the two managers.

Negative Inquiry can be used several times in a conversation and can be alternated with Fogging to accomplish the desired end result for the victim of the aggressive assault. "What aspect of the mistake is most bothersome to you?" "What consequence of the misinformation is of greatest concern to you right now?"

Telling What You Want

A very direct approach is often not so good with an aggressive communicator in assault mode, but you could try an adaptation of Telling What You Want if you're brave.

This advanced technique produces a content-to-process switch. You want to switch the focus from the attacking content to the communication process between you and the aggressive communicator. The goal is to change the direction of the conversation—to get it out of attack mode, to move it into problem-solving mode, or to end it.

Part of the reason that this approach works is that it's unexpected and breaks out of the usual patterns for this kind of confrontive conversation. It may put the aggressive communicator off balance slightly, which is in your best interest, the attackee's.

This kind of intervention can take place at any point in a confrontive conversation, but the earlier the better. You want to make sure that you say it before you get feeling so beaten up that you can't do it. Here's what Telling What You Want as a content-to-process switch might look like in the Sam scenario. It could take place at any point. Either Glynda or Neil could do it. Early on in the conversation, Neil might say, "I'm uncomfortable when you don't let us finish our explanation after you've asked us to tell you what happened. I'd like to be able to say what I have to say without being interrupted." Neil changes the focus from the content, the screwup, to the process, the conversation between the three people.

Later in the conversation Glynda could say, "Sam, I feel attacked when you tell me that I'm an idiot and don't have a clue about what's going on. I'd like to move on and talk about what we need to do now about the problem." Glynda is suggesting that the direction of the conversation change from talking about the mistake, and specifically about her and Neil, to talking about solutions. Or Neil could say, "I don't appreciate your interrupting me and saying you don't care if I'm sick. I'd like the opportunity to tell you what I'm thinking about the situation without being cut off." Again, Neil is switching from the content to the process.

The worst that can happen under these circumstances is that your Telling What You Want comment is tramped on or ignored. Sam might say, "I don't care what you want. I'm running the show here." He might not even respond to what you say and just keep on rampaging or interrupt you again to say, "BS" or some other equally as resistant comment. You will still feel better than if you sit there quietly and get squashed or if you mount a counterattack.

But if Sam does ignore, rampage, or interrupt, you can use one of two other techniques if you're still breathing. You can use Broken Record and say the same thing over again in a slightly different way:

"I would like to start talking about solutions instead of focus-
    ing only on the problem."
"I want to finish what I'm saying."
"I'd like you to let me continue what I was saying."

An escalation of the Telling What You Want technique is to add a consequence if your request isn't met the first time. Rev up your courage quotient for this next step. If Sam runs over you, you can then say, "Sam, I told you I wanted to finish saying what I have to say. The next time I'm interrupted, I'm going to leave because there's no communication going on." Or, "Sam, I said I preferred to start talking about solutions. If you continue to talk about what idiots Neil and I are, I'm going to leave. I'll meet with you anytime that you want to talk about how we're going to deal with the problem from this point on." Although this kind of approach seems terrifying to nonassertive communicators, the aggressive person may respect the clear confident message that's being sent. He or she won't tell you they respect your approach, however. You may decide to try the consequence addendum only after you've been successful several times with some of the other techniques suggested.

Regardless of what you choose to do and say, don't expect the aggressive communicator to apologize, to tell you that he gets it and is changing his ways, that he sees the light and is reforming. Most aggressive people won't give you the satisfaction of being right even if they think you are right. They may change their behavior somewhat, but they won't give you credit for it, publicly or privately, so don't wait. Just be confident if you have had an impact and they decrease their intensity by a notch. That's a real win for you, even if a low visibility win

Remember

Communicating with an aggressive person is difficult for most people. Few individuals enjoy confrontation and most are scared by a hostile, loud manner. Give yourself a lot of leeway and support in dealing with these tough types. Work slowly to improve your skills and confidence in coping with their harsh style.

- The most important change you can make is to learn to alter your negative thinking so that you can stay calm in the face of an assault.
- Eliminate apologies, defenses, justifications, qualifiers. They don't help.
- As you get more confident in staying calm, you can try out Fogging and Negative Inquiry. They are both good techniques to use when you want to buy time, stay nondefensive, and interrupt the prevailing pattern.
- The content-to-process switch, using Telling What You Want as a technique, is an advanced approach for dealing with the aggressive communicator that you might want to try after you feel good about using Fogging and Negative Inquiry.

- Be satisfied with feeling relatively intact after an aggressive attack, rather than hoping or waiting for your aggressive boss to see the light, come to his senses, and tell you
  that you're right and the best!

11

A Day in the Life of the "I Mean Business" Communicator

There are hundreds of opportunities in any given day to be assertive at home and at work. When the opportunities are taken, you can save hours of time, preserve relationships, increase productivity and harmony, decrease stress, and even have more fun. Using great communication most of the time makes life smoother, easier, and more comfortable. You learn that you can count on yourself to avoid disastrous situations and to escape catastrophic communication that someone else tries to drag you into. Your internal dialogue improves, your confidence grows, and you live happily ever after!

Starting with an average day on the job, let's look at all the times you can use assertiveness either as an initiator or a responder during a normal day.

It's a Thursday morning. Staff meeting at 7:30 A.M. You're the new team leader and you're already a bit worried. Your internal dialogue is whirling. "Will Raul show up late as always? Who's going to give me a hard time? I'm not sure I can run these meetings very well. Maybe I should get someone from HR to help me with this next time. I hate having all this responsibility. I've got to be sure that I don't let my impatience with Cindy show. I wish I didn't have to do this. I don't present very well."

Wait a minute! You catch yourself in the midst of this negative thinking and remember to Substitute, Challenge, and Stop. You remember a substitute statement that usually works well for you. "Keep the focus on the present; what is it I have to do?" Then you remember another one. "One step at a time: I can handle the situation." You block out the negativity, focus on preparing for the meeting, do some problem-solving thinking, and immediately feel better.

Everyone begins to filter into the meeting room. There's quiet conversation going on, but the atmosphere seems a little tense. You start wondering what's wrong. Off goes the internal monologue again. "Uh oh. What's the matter? Are they mad at me? Is someone going to hand me really bad news during his report?" You catch the internal speech more quickly this time and remind yourself that right now you need to just be pleasant and friendly and say a few words to each team member as he arrives.

You were right. Raul is late. You start the meeting on time

anyway. But you decide that rather than stewing during the meeting about Raul's lateness, you'll make the decision now about how to handle the problem. Dealing with the Raul lateness issue publicly in the meeting probably isn't a good idea. The team is brand-new and doesn't really know yet how to function as a team, so they won't bring it up. You decide to say publicly, before the meeting ends, that you'd like to talk to Raul briefly after the meeting. That way the rest of the team will know that you're paying attention. You'll figure out what and how you're going to communicate to Raul later. Right now you need to start the meeting with some energy.

"Good morning. Let's get started. I'd like to change the format of the meeting from the one that we've been using, going around the table and having everyone say what's new or what's a problem. Here's my idea. Since we are working on functioning as a team instead of a chain of command, I think the focus of the meeting should be on the team member who has the highest priority problem to solve or the highest priority information to disseminate. That requires each of you to take more initiative, rather than my calling on each of you in turn, but it seems a more effective use of our time. I'd like to hear your thoughts about the suggested change in format."

As you listen to people's comments you are able to acknowledge a good idea with an "I" statement:

"I appreciate your bringing that point out."
"I think your suggestion is key to making this change successfully."

You use Fogging and Negative Inquiry to deal with team members' criticism of the idea:

"Maybe I did spring it on you too fast."
"Perhaps we should walk through a sample meeting before we actually agree to do it the new way."
"What concerns you about prioritizing problems, Carl?"

After listening to comments, encouraging participation from everyone present, and noting the expected resistance to change, you say, "I think walking through a sample meeting in the new way at next week's staff meeting is a great way to gather information about whether we want to make this change. We'll plan to do that."

The meeting continues in its usual pattern. Raul does come in late and you say, "Good morning" to him but don't address the lateness issue. Just before closing the meeting you say, "I'd like to meet with you for a minute after the meeting, Raul." When team members have left, you address Raul: "I'm frustrated with your coming to this morning's meeting twenty minutes late, and I'd like you to be on time. I'd like you to write down for me some suggestions for solving the lateness issue before it becomes a real performance problem." You listen as Raul explains this morning's lateness, and then, using Broken Record, say, "I want to work on solving the lateness problem. Let me know your thoughts on solutions before the end of the week."

You're feeling pretty good about yourself as Raul leaves. So far, so good. But the day always holds unexpected interruptions and crises that you can't prepare for mentally or verbally. Those are the tough times. When you can plan ahead and know the difficulty you have to handle, you're more likely to succeed. You know you have a touchy situation coming up.

An angry customer called yesterday, complaining about poor service. He demanded to talk to you, but you weren't available. You told the supervisor to tell him that you would definitely call him back this morning. Now you must do it. Your negative thinking is going bananas, and you can feel a knot in your stomach and some shortness of breath. You write several good substitute statements and attach them to your desk, near the telephone.

"Just breathe deeply."
"I've survived this and worse before."
"He's telling me something about him, he's not telling me something about me."
"This tenseness can be an ally, a cue to cope."

You say a couple of these coping statements to yourself.

You make the call, hoping he'll be out, but of course he's

there and sounds angry when he says, "Hello." "Good morning, Mr. Grossman. This is Connie Crisopoulos calling, the manager you wanted to speak to at Bondy's Office Equipment." Mr. Grossman flies off into an angry harangue about bad service, rude receptionists, incorrect information, and malfunctioning equipment.

The first approach you always take when a customer is angry is to listen very carefully and acknowledge his or her comments occasionally, without interrupting. As you listen, you also are saying those great coping statements to yourself to keep out the catastrophic negative thinking and to keep you functioning well and thinking clearly.

When he seems to have run down, you use some Fogging. "We certainly could have handled the situation much better than we did." Some Negative Inquiry works well too. "What aspect of the whole transaction was the most bothersome to you, Mr. Grossman?"

In this situation you remember to eliminate disclaimers and apologies, the excessive words, details, and explanations that would tend to further annoy this customer. "Mr. Grossman, I am disappointed that you've had this bad experience with our company. I'd like to know what I can do at this time to improve the situation and decrease your frustration." Surprisingly, Mr. Grossman tells you exactly what you can do and tells you that he wants you and only you to take care of the problem because he doesn't have faith in anyone else at this point. You're amazed, but tell him that you will take care of it and will call him back when you have the specifics about time and date for pickup of his fax machine and delivery and installation of a new machine. You tell him that you'll be there in person.

When you get off the phone, you're feeling good about how you handled the situation. You were brief, concise, and professional. You weren't defensive or overly solicitous. You're just about to tell your friend and coworker about your accomplishment when the volume on the old negative thinking is turned up:

"You were way too wimpy with him."
"You can't go on deliveries every time someone is unhappy with their new office equipment. Are you crazy?"

"How can I keep this from my boss? He won't be happy."
"Was that assertive? Or was that really nonassertive? Did I really mess that up?"

But within three minutes, you recognize you're into a self-defeating pattern. You switch gears and come up with a by-now familiar and comfortable coping statement. "I'm pleased with the progress I'm making." You say it over and over to yourself until you've blocked out the negativity and you believe your new monologue. Hooray! Another tiny triumph!

Just as you're savoring your success, one of those interruptions that you've learned to expect happens. Sarita, one of your team members, knocks timidly on the cubicle wall and asks if she could have a minute of your time. You invite her to sit down and tell her, "I can talk for five minutes, but I have a staff meeting with Lowell at eleven. If you would like more time, we can schedule it for later today."

You feel good about initiating the conversation in this way. You've found yourself too many times in the middle of a big problem discussion with someone when you have to be somewhere else. Then you're in a no-win. You either leave them in the middle of their emotional issue or you're late for the meeting that you have scheduled. Now, you've learned to directly tell them up front so they can make the decision that's best for them. If their need is for brief information, they can ask and you can tell. If their need is for more coaching or counseling, they can let you know and reschedule.

You and Sarita schedule a twenty-minute appointment for later in the day. You're concerned as you go off to your meeting with your boss, because Sarita looks tired and sounds bummed out. You put it out of your mind and remember, "Focus on the present. What is it I have to do now?"

The staff meeting with your boss is always somewhat difficult for you because the rest of his direct reports are all men. Even though you have a good relationship with them, they all seem so loud, direct, and confident in the meetings that you attend together that you end up shutting down. Then they all hassle you, in a joking manner, about not participating and not being a good team player.

You've decided to handle it differently today. You're going to speak up early in the meeting; the first chance you get, if only to hear yourself say some words and break the spell. You know it'll be easier to keep on making comments after the first shot is fired. You also know that the men will give you a lot of grief about anything you say. They'll joke and tease good-naturedly, but you can be disconcerted and embarrassed by the flak. Sometimes you end up shutting down. You don't want that to happen again today. .

You've set a clear, specific goal: to speak up within the first five minutes of the meeting, and to say something every fifteen minutes until the meeting is over, regardless of whether you get a positive or negative response. You've got your head in a good place. You're not going to take stuff personally. You're going to say to yourself, "They're telling me something about them. They're not telling me something about me." The substitute thinking helps create some distance between you and the flak, so you can be more courageous. It's like putting on a bulletproof vest for the meeting. It protects you, but doesn't necessarily show. That's another technique you can use. Visualize yourself at the meeting, protected by a clear plastic guard in front of you. When the comments and jokes, the teasing put-downs hit, they bounce off without touching you.

You're ready to do it. You've chosen techniques to use. You're just going to use a sequence of "I" statements. You'll be brief and specific. You arrive a little early so you have time to converse, to make eye contact, and to get comfortable with people before the meeting starts. You know from experience that your preference has been to arrive at the last minute, slip into place silently, and be invisible. But you also know that the old approach doesn't work to give you the oomph you need to speak up. Within the first five minutes of the meeting, as the Marketing guy finishes making his comments, you say, "I'd like to talk with you more about the marketing customer service connection. I have some ideas." He responds, "Let's set it up after this meeting." Nobody looks at you strangely, or says anything, or teases you about suggesting that you had some ideas. The situation is almost anticlimactic.

Discussion continues on a variety of topics: scheduling, hiring a consultant, problems, budget. You continue to add brief "I" statements. "I agree with you, Dave." "I had that same problem with Accounts Receivable. Wanda ended up being the most knowledgeable and helpful person there." Everything is going along well. You're beginning to think you don't need the vest or the plastic guard. You're feeling confident and courageous. You take a bigger step. "I'd like to suggest that we run a couple of focus groups to get better information from our present customers. Customer Service could do it, Marketing could do it, or we both could do it in conjunction with HR."

Nobody says anything, almost as if they hadn't heard what you said, and the conversation continues. Suddenly, you feel vulnerable and invisible again. You definitely take this personally. The internal monologue starts up with a vengeance:

"They must think that's a pretty stupid idea to not even respond to it."
"Why are they ignoring me?"
"Well, this isn't working at all. What am I doing wrong?"

You feel yourself shrinking in your chair. Then you catch yourself and get a grip!

"Wait a minute. They're telling me something about them, not about me." As you snap out of your brief slump, you realize that they ignore each other's ideas as well. The problem-solving approach seems to be unfocused. People are just throwing out ideas, but discussion isn't taking place. There seems to be a competitive rather than a cooperative atmosphere.

Once you figure out that what's going on is definitely not personal, your mind frees up to address solutions. You're not sure where to go. Should you restate your idea, but louder, and interrupt them as they're interrupting each other? Should you just relax now that you see it's not a personal thing? Should you say something about the process that you see going on? Or would that sound like you were trying to be in control? Or would you sound like a teacher?

You go back to basics. "What do I want?" You remember that what you want is to speak up more often and not take the responses too personally. You have done that and you want to continue doing that. You pat yourself on the back for what you've already done and decide that you want to make a comment about the group process. Your negative thinking revs up, but you challenge it quickly. "What's the worst thing that can possibly happen? They ignore me again. Or they tell me my idea is stupid. How can I handle that? I'll just put on the vest and put up the plastic guard before I say anything and I'll say to myself, 'I've dealt with worse situations before.' "

Well-armed, you say loudly, for you, "I think we could handle this more efficiently. Let's pick two of the best ideas, ask two people to volunteer to flesh out the ideas and bring them back to our meeting next week." Everyone does not stand up and give you a standing ovation for a great idea! Actually they don't say anything to you. But they do start doing what you suggested. Whew! You breathe an internal sigh of relief.

The meeting continues uneventfully. You make a few comments here or there, with little in the way of response. Actually, you're even missing some of the joking and teasing that you get when you're quieter. You're not sure what the response, or lack of it, means, but you're clear that you're not going to waste time analyzing, interpreting, or generally stewing about it. You did what you set out to do. That's what's important.

When the meeting is finally over, you decide to reward yourself. You've done a good job all day, particularly in this last meeting, which is generally so tough for you. You decide you need to find a female friend to talk to. You want to tell someone else who'll understand just how well you've done and how hard it was. But you're not going to ask her to help you figure out exactly what the men's behavior meant. You're going to let go of that. Over coffee and a cinnamon roll in the cafeteria you extol your virtues. You've warned your friend Jan. "I'm going to be self-centered today. I want to brag about the communication changes I've made and I want you to tell me how terrific I am! This break is part of my reward system."

Jan knows you well and understands entirely. She has less trouble than you in her communication, but she does appreciate the struggle you're having and the improvements you've made. You tell her how much you appreciate her. "I feel really good that you took fifteen minutes to get together and listen. I'd like to do the same for you when it fits." She acknowledges that she'll definitely take you up on your offer.

Back to the office you go, feeling energized and up. The hard stuff is out of the way for the day. Now all you have to do is meet with Sarita, finish some paperwork and phone calls. Nothing scary, nothing requiring brilliance and courage. You do want to get the odds and ends finished up so you can leave by 5:30 because you're meeting a friend for dinner and a movie.

The meeting with Sarita takes place in your office. Although you're not sure what she wants, you do know what you want. You want the meeting to be solution-oriented, and you want Sarita to leave with the monkey of responsibility for action on her and not on you. You realize that how you communicate is the key to how she leaves the meeting.

"Sarita, let's start out by your telling me briefly what your concern is." Sarita goes into a long, detailed story about family health problems involving her daughters and her mother, who stays with the children while Sarita is at work. You want to be empathetic and you want the conversation to move to the bottom line. You say, "I'd like to know what effect you see this concern having for you at work."

Again, Sarita starts talking in detail about how stressed she is, how tired she is because she can't sleep, and how hard the situation is to handle. Using a form of Broken Record, you say, "At work, what problems is this causing you and what needs to happen?" She says she doesn't know. You tell her that you see that she's going through a stressful time, but that she must be more specific about what she needs from you or the team or the company. She still doesn't seem to be able to answer. You're beginning to feel responsible. You feel the guilt creeping in as you get a mental picture of Sarita's two young daughters with asthma, coughing and thin. You remind yourself before your negative thinking gets out of control, "I have a responsibility toward Sarita, but I'm not responsible for her." You suggest that she talk to a counselor in the employee assistance program today. You ask her to get back to you tomorrow and let you know what was decided. Sarita looks disappointed. You're not sure what she expected from you, but you feel OK about your conversation.

When you walk out of your office with Sarita, the boss's secretary looks up as you pass and says, "He's looking for you. That was a pretty fast disappearing act you made after the staff meeting. A power nap in your car?" You tighten up immediately and start to get angry. There she goes spoiling the glow. What is she trying to do? You catch yourself feeling defensive and recognize the good old indirect assault. It's a little one, from a frequent source, but you decide to handle it differently today. Normally you would start defending yourself. "I was just having coffee in the cafeteria. I was only gone for fifteen minutes. What's the problem? Is he still here? Where is he? Should I just go looking for him?" You would give away your power to her. Not this time. You answer matter-of-factly as you pass by, "I'll be in my office the rest of the afternoon." You figure that if your boss is still in the vicinity, he'll ask or look for you again. If not, he'll find you when he comes back.

You use the plain old Stop technique to keep from obsessing about what your boss might or might not want to see you about. There really is no reason to think there's a problem. You get on with the paperwork and phone calls and feel good about letting go of the negative internal monologue. You are really focused and productive. Getting rid of the garbage thinking produces amazing results.

An hour later, your boss sticks his head in your door. "Connie, I need to talk to you about a new, big, exciting project. I've got to head to another meeting now, but I'll catch you when I get back around 5 or 5:30." You notice some urgency in his voice. But you've got plans for tonight. You're thinking, he's leaving. What to do? You don't know but you don't want to just let the decision be made by your passivity.

Quickly you mentally say, "What do I want?" and answer, "I don't know." So you get up and say, "I'll walk with you to your meeting." You still don't quite know what to say or do. You're not sure what his priorities are, how important the new project is, how long he wants to meet with you. You don't know if your insisting on leaving at 5:30 as planned is being assertive or pig-headed. You suddenly do know what you want. You want the meeting in the morning. If he thinks the conversation is essential now, he'll tell you.

"Lowell, I'd prefer to meet first thing in the morning if you're available." He responds, "Sure, I can be here at 7:30, can you?" "That would work out well," you respond. As he heads off for his meeting he says jokingly, "You'll be sorry you didn't meet today. I know you. You probably won't be able to sleep because you'll be so worried about what this project is all about. You better not be late in the morning and then tell me you overslept!"

He does know you well. At least the old you. But surprisingly, you're not so worried. If getting together was truly urgent, he would have insisted. Actually, rather than feeling worried, you're excited about hearing the news in the morning. But more than that, you're feeling great and free because you've done what you said you wanted to do under many different circumstances. And it wasn't that tough. You can really say to yourself, "I Mean Business," and know you finally do.

12
What's Next?

Once you've learned to be a good, direct, open communicator and have practiced your new skills in a variety of settings, simple to complex, you must be feeling good! Knowing that you can speak up rather than stew, say "no" rather than make up a hundred excuses, or tell people how you feel and what you want is mind-boggling. Giving up nonassertiveness is like giving up any bad habit—it's freeing. You have much more time and energy as an assertive person. You waste much less of both by not worrying, not fearing, not overplanning, or wondering or guessing what to do, not concerning yourself with what other people think, or what the consequences of your words will be.

Maintenance

Generally, maintaining the new thinking and communication habits isn't difficult because the new ways are so intrinsically rewarding. They're also extrinsically rewarding if you continue to use the IMB MO and reward yourself for trying out some new techniques and for taking risks rather than rewarding yourself only for perfection and success. You feel more comfortable and confident in interpersonal situations. You also feel better when you're alone with yourself because you're not wasting time with recriminations or reenactments or unfinished business or leftover conflict.

Externally life usually goes better as well. As you act more assertive and communicate more directly, people treat you with a renewed respect. As they treat you with more respect, your confidence increases and you're more able to continue being assertive. You're more able to improve your skills and move on to more difficult situations with even tougher people. As one of my class participants said, "I'm getting drunk with power! I'm turning into an assertiveness maniac!"

Sometimes people learning a new skill or technique of any kind do overcompensate before they move back toward the middle. In my experience, overcompensating is definitely better than undercompensating. In order to change, people often have to make a dramatic leap and expenditure of energy to get their feet out of the concrete. They may settle in a place they don't necessarily want to stay, but their feet aren't stuck in the old concrete or yet immersed in the new. They can still move around readily. Another factor contributing to the value of overcompensating is the reaction of friends, families, and coworkers to your change. Usually the people who know you have become very comfortable with a certain pattern of communication and behavior that exists between you and them. The pattern is predictable. It's comfortable and almost goes on automatically. Here's a common old pattern:

Kareem:	"Tonya, I need these twenty-five faxes sent out by noon. Also call all the members of the diversity committee and tell them the meeting date has been changed to the second Monday instead of the first. I'll be back at noon and need your input on the Baxter report on my desk."
Tonya:	(with a pleading-for-understanding look): "Kareem, I'd really like to help you with all that stuff but I've got so much to do, I'm not even sure I can get to the Baxter report by noon."
Kareem:	"Tonya, you know I count on you to pitch in when I get in a bind like this. This meeting I have with Jim is very important. I'd do the same for you. Come on. Please. This really will be the last time I ask."
Tonya:	"OK. You win. I'll try. But please don't ask me again. I just can't keep on getting all your stuff and my stuff done."
Kareem:	"It's not your stuff and my stuff. It's our stuff!"

A different way of stating the pattern between Kareem and Tonya is:

Kareem:	Tells what help he needs in a way that assumes compliance.
Tonya:	Says nonassertively that she doesn't have time.
Kareem:	Uses urgency, guilt induction, and promise to never repeat the pattern in order to get Tonya's compliance.
Tonya:	Gives in.

> *Kareem:*   Is appreciative, but emphasizes that she's doing it for them, not him.

Usually such a pattern develops and is maintained by each person knowing exactly what's going to happen, perhaps on a less than fully conscious level. Everyone just plays his or her role to the inevitable expected outcome.

When one person changes his part in the play, the other person has to change her part, although at first they may go on as if the play and the parts and the lines haven't changed. Let's look at what might happen the first time Tonya changes her lines.

> *Kareem:*   "Tonya, I need these twenty-five faxes sent out by noon. Also call all the members of the diversity committee and tell them the meeting date has been changed to the second Monday instead of the first. I'll be back at noon and need your input on the Baxter report on my desk. (Old pattern)
>
> *Tonya:*   "Kareem, no to the faxes and the calls. Yes to the Baxter report by noon." (New response)
>
> *Kareem:*   "Tonya, you know I count on you to pitch in when I get in a bind like this. You know how important this meeting I have with Jim is. I'd do the same for you. Come on. Please. This really will be the last time I ask." (Old pattern)
>
> *Tonya:*   "I promise the Baxter report. That's it." (New response)
>
> *Kareem:*   Well, don't ask me for help anymore. You won't get it. (New response)

The pattern is broken. After two different responses by Tonya, Kareem can't stay in the routine. He has to alter his lines. Tonya would of course prefer that he alter his response in a more positive way, but by changing her response, she inevitably changes his. He may try again, another day or time, to get the pattern back. If Tonya goes back to the old response, feeling guilty and trying to make up for saying "no" last time or hoping

Kareem will understand, she's stuck again. If instead Tonya continues the new pattern, eventually Kareem will stop asking her to do extra work, or his work, unless he has a true emergency. After setting a consistent new pattern, Tonya can afford to help in an emergency or even offer some help on a day when she has time and Kareem clearly doesn't.

Maintaining your new pattern is enhanced by working with someone else who's working on assertive communication skills. She'll be a good source of coaching and reward, as you will be for her. She'll also help you deal with the inevitable fear or concern that may descend on you when you've done a good job, succeeded in attaining what you wanted to do, but your message was not received enthusiastically. Changing a habit a health habit, a work habit, or a communication habit—is always easier if you have someone else to compete and collaborate with!

What's Next?

Of course you can't just settle in and be comfortable and enjoy your new communication skills! As Martin Seligman, Ph.D., says in his excellent book, *What You Can Change . . . And What You Can't*, the culture of the United States is one of the few that historically emphasizes the importance, the possibility, and the desirability of ongoing, continual self-improvement. Seligman says that we all need to do a better job of accepting ourselves as we are in certain areas that we truly can't change. But the improvement of communication skills doesn't fit under the category of behaviors or characteristics that are unchangeable!

Beyond Assertiveness

Once you've become a comfortable, confident, assertive, direct communicator, you can begin to think about broadening your repertoire even further, by learning and using indirect influence skills. I group the indirect communication skills under the heading of Beyond Assertiveness, to distinguish them from Before Assertiveness.

Before Assertiveness, there were many comments you didn't make, "noes" you didn't say, feelings you didn't express, and wants you didn't ask for. Often you weren't in a position to choose whether to do or say what you wanted to because you were too fearful or you didn't know how.

Now that you have learned to overcome your fears and have acquired some good communication techniques, you can make choices about how to handle a situation. Now there may be situations in which you choose to make no comment, say no "noes," keep your feelings to yourself, and not ask for what you want. You may make that choice because it seems a more effective strategy to get what you want in that situation.

When you're dealing with a very resistant, oppositional, or hostile audience of one or many, being open, honest, and direct isn't effective. I recently facilitated a small group of managers who up front, directly told me that they were going to give me a hard time, that they didn't like warm fuzzy anything, that they didn't think I had anything to offer, and that they had a history of being tough on presenters! The open, honest, and direct approach with these managers would be to start out my meeting with them by saying, "I feel uncomfortable about your stated lack of enthusiasm and interest in our working together on this project today. I would like you to consider the possibility that the time will be very well spent and that your active participation will make this worthwhile for everyone." I knew I could say that, or any other variation of a direct, open comment to them at the beginning of the meeting. But I didn't think it would work to get what I wanted—their active participation and some interest and enthusiasm in the project. I didn't want the meeting to turn into a power struggle—them against me.

I chose instead to use an indirect communication strategy, a Beyond Assertiveness approach to get their cooperation. I used a technique I call the Confusion Technique. I started out by telling them that I knew they were a results-oriented group who could accomplish whatever they wanted, once they decided what they wanted to do. I said that in the four hours we had together they could accomplish the task of working together cooperatively and could probably accomplish that task in less than four hours if they chose to. I said that they also might choose not to work together cooperatively. Since the group was so results-oriented, they could also accomplish that goal effectively, but it would probably take more than four hours. The group was confused and amused. I was no longer the opposition. They saw that the choice of rebelling or cooperating was truly theirs and would benefit or harm only them, not me. The approach worked, in this situation, with this group, much more effectively than an assertive approach.

Because you are saying or not saying what you want out of choice, rather than out of fear, using Beyond Assertiveness, you experience the situation entirely differently. You come across in a different manner, and people's response to you is very different.

There are a variety of situations in which an indirect approach may work more effectively for you than the direct approach of Assertive Communication. But you'll only feel confident enough to choose indirectness when you're experienced at being open, honest, and direct first. So get on out there and start now. Start with the easiest and move up to the hardest situations. Remember the IMB MO and use it systematically. Never forget to reward yourself before you evaluate yourself. And don't forget to have fun!

Appendix

Self-Statements for Dealing With Anger

This is going to upset me, but I know how to deal with it.
I can work out a plan to handle this.
If I find myself getting upset, I'll know what to do.
This could be a testy situation, but I believe in myself.
As long as I keep my cool, I'm in control.
I don't have to prove myself.
Don't make more out of this than I have to.
For someone to be that irritable, he must be awfully unhappy.
If I start to get angry, I'll just be banging my head against the wall.
My muscles are starting to feel tight. Time to relax and slow down.
I have a right to be annoyed, but let's keep the lid on.
Let's take the issues point by point.
I'm not going to get pushed around, but I'm not going haywire either.
I can't expect people to act the way I want them to.

Self-Support for Unresolved Conflict

These are difficult situations, and they take time to straighten out.

Try to shake it off. Don't let it interfere with my job.
I'll get better at this as I get more practice.
Don't take it personally.

Self-Support for Resolved Conflict or Successful Coping

I handled that one pretty well. It worked!
It could have been a lot worse.
I'm doing better at this all the time.

Self-Statements for Dealing With Stress

What is it I have to do?
Just think about it. That's better than getting anxious.
No negative self-statements; just think rationally.
Don't worry; worry won't help anything.
I can convince myself to do it; I can reason my fear away.
One step at a time; I can handle the situation.
This tenseness can be an ally, a cue to cope.
When fear comes, just pause; take a deep breath.
Keep the focus on the present; what is it I have to do?
I should expect my fear to rise.
Don't try to eliminate fear totally; just keep it manageable.

Self-Congratulations

It worked; I did it!
It wasn't as bad as I expected.
I made more out of my fear than it was worth.
I can be pleased with the progress I'm making.

Self-Statements for Preparing for Difficult Situations

There's nothing to worry about.
I'm going to be all right.
I've succeeded with this before.
What exactly do I have to do?
I know I can do each one of these tasks.
It's easier once you get started.
I'll jump in and be all right.

Tomorrow I'll be through it.
Don't let negative thoughts creep in.

Self-Statements for Confronting the Difficult Situation

Stay organized.
Take it step by step, don't rush.
I can do this, I'm doing it now.
I can only do my best.
Any tension I feel is a signal to use my coping exercises.
I can get help if I need it.
If I don't think about fear, I won't be afraid.
If I get tense, I'll take a breather and relax.
It's OK to make mistakes.

Self-Statements for Coping With Emotional Arousal

Relax now!
Just breathe deeply.
There's an end to it.
Keep my mind on right now, on the task at hand.
I can keep this within limits I can handle.
I can always call _____.
I am only afraid because I decided to be. I can decide not
   to be.
I've survived this and worse before.
Being active will lessen the fear.

Self-Statements for Reinforcing Success

I did it!
I did all right. I did well.
Next time I won't have to worry as much.
I am able to relax away anxiety.
I've got to tell _____ about this.
It's possible not to be scared. All I have to do is stop think-
   ing I'm scared.

Adapted from D. Meichenbaum and M. Jaremko, *Stress Reduction and Prevention* (New York: Plenum, 1983).

Bibliography

Alberti, R. and M. Emmons. *Your Perfect Right: A Guide to Assertive Living.* Sixth Ed. San Luis Obispo, California: Impact Publishers, 1990.

Bandler, R. and J. Grinder. *Reframing.* Moab, Utah: Real People Press, 1982, p. 1.

Bloom, L., K. Coburn and J. Pearlman. *The New Assertive Woman.* New York: Dell Publishing, 1975.

Dailey, P. "Diversity: What Has Communication Got to Do With It?" *Managing Diversity.* Fredonia, New York: Jamestown Area Labor Management Committee Inc., vol. 4, no. 9, June 1995, p. 5.

Dauten, D., "Business' Underused Tool: 'No.' " *The Arizona Republic,* July 30, 1995, p. F10.

Eisen, J. with P. Farley. *Powertalk!* New York: Simon and Schuster, 1984.

Guralnik, D., *Webster's New World Dictionary.* New York: Simon and Schuster, 1984.

Kreitner, R. and A. Kinicki. *Organizational Behavior.* Instructor's ed. Homewood, Illinois: Irwin, 1992.

Lange, A. and P. Jakubowski. *Responsible Assertive Behavior.* Champaign, Illinois: Research Press, 1978.

Mann, J. "To Help Girls, We Must Raise Boys Differently." *The Arizona Republic,* March 5, 1995, p. F1.

Meichenbaum, D. *Cognitive-Behavior Modification.* New York: Plenum Press, 1977.

Meichenbaum, D. and M. Jaremko. *Stress Reduction and Prevention*. New York: Fawcett Columbine, 1993.

Smith, M. *When I Say No, I Feel Guilty*. New York: Bantam Books, 1975.

Tingley, J. *Genderflex™: Men and Women Speaking Each Other's Language at Work*. New York: AMACOM, 1994.

Wolpe, Joseph, and Arnold Lazarus. *Behavior Therapy Techniques*. New York: Pergamon Press, 1966.

Index